COLOR ALL THE SHAPES IN DIFFERENT COLORS

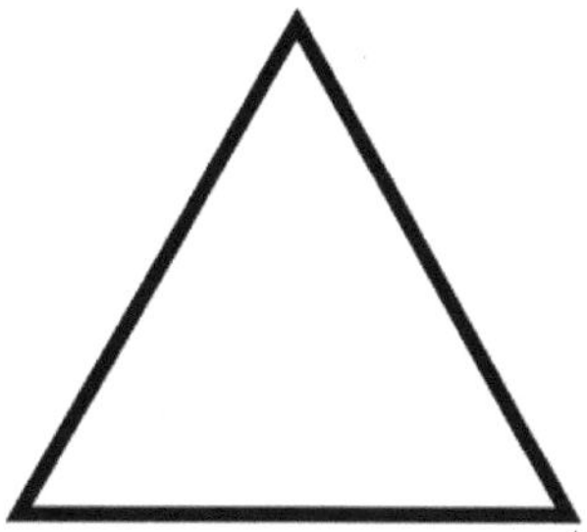

TRIANGLE

SQUARE

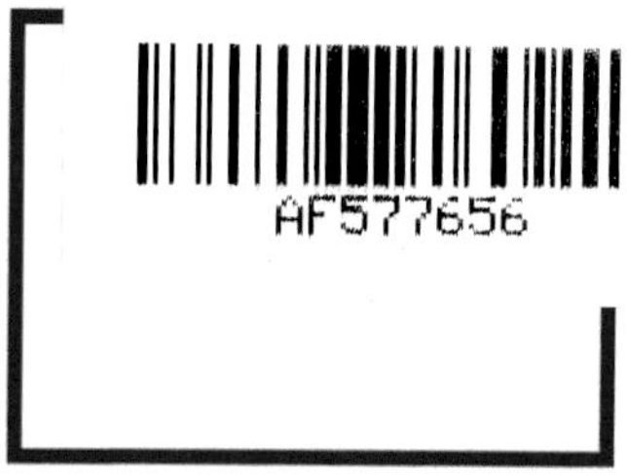

RECTANGLE

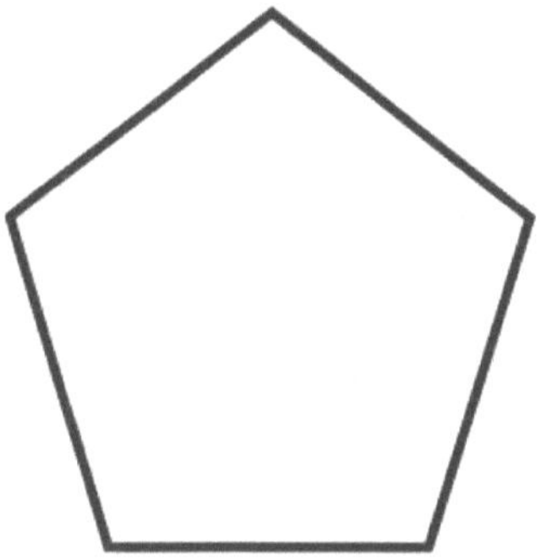

PENTAGON

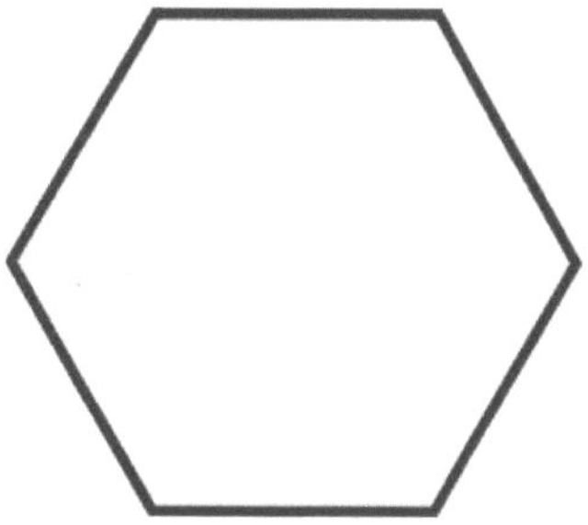

HEXAGON

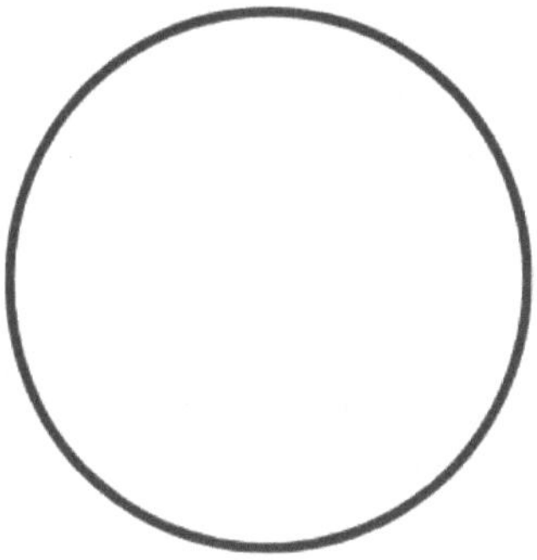

CIRCLE

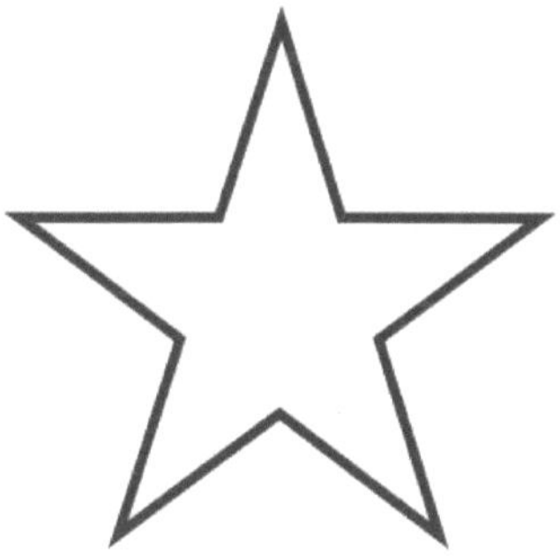

STAR

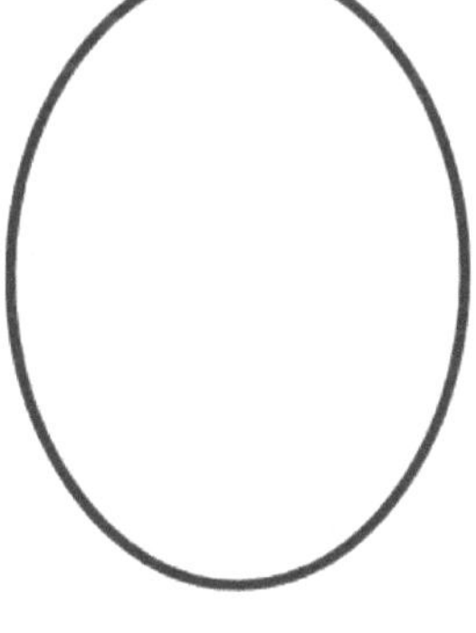

OVAL

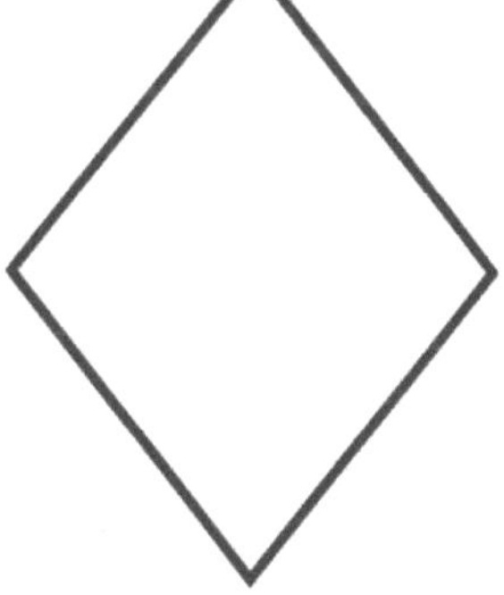

DIAMOND

clever projects

FIND AND COLOR THE CIRCLES

FINISH THE PICTURE

WHAT IS HIDING BEHIND THE CIRCLE ?

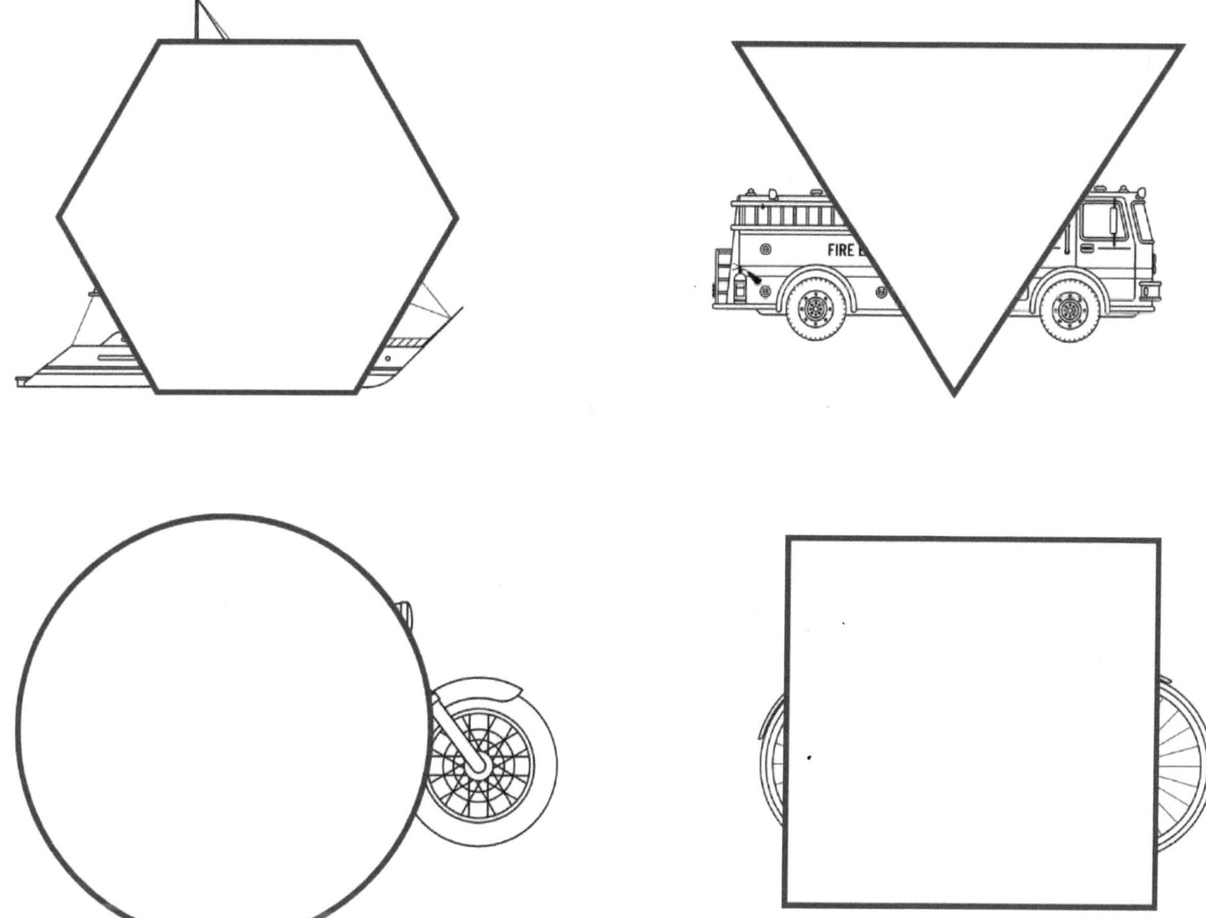

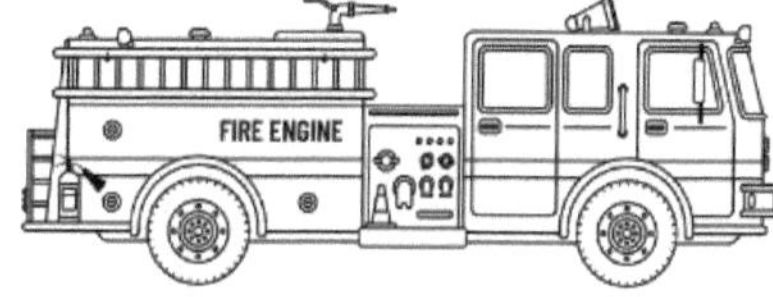

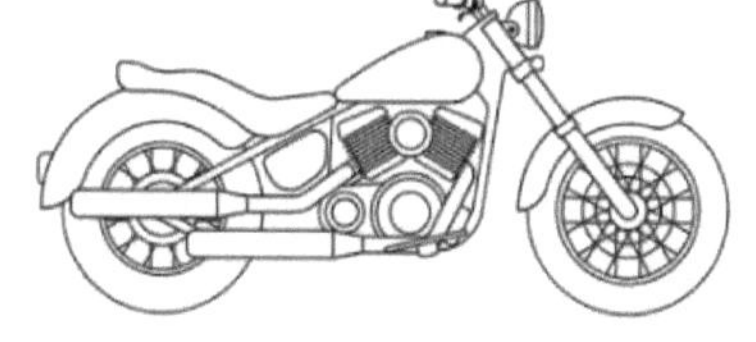

FIND THE ROW OF SHAPES IN THE PICTURE BELOW AND CIRCLE IT

CUT THE SHAPE WITH SCISSORS

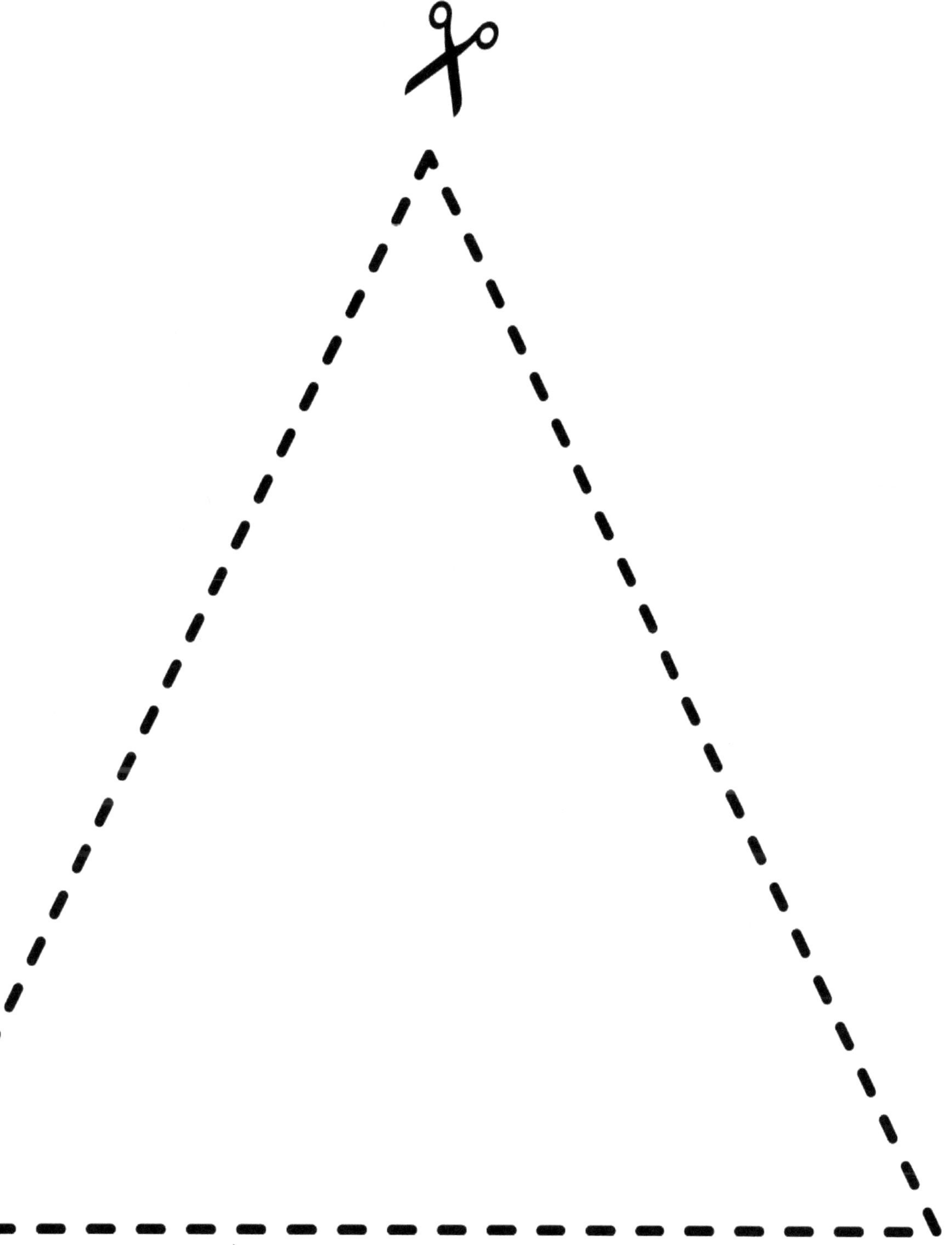

DRAW THE SHAPE WITH BOTH HANDS AT THE SAME TIME

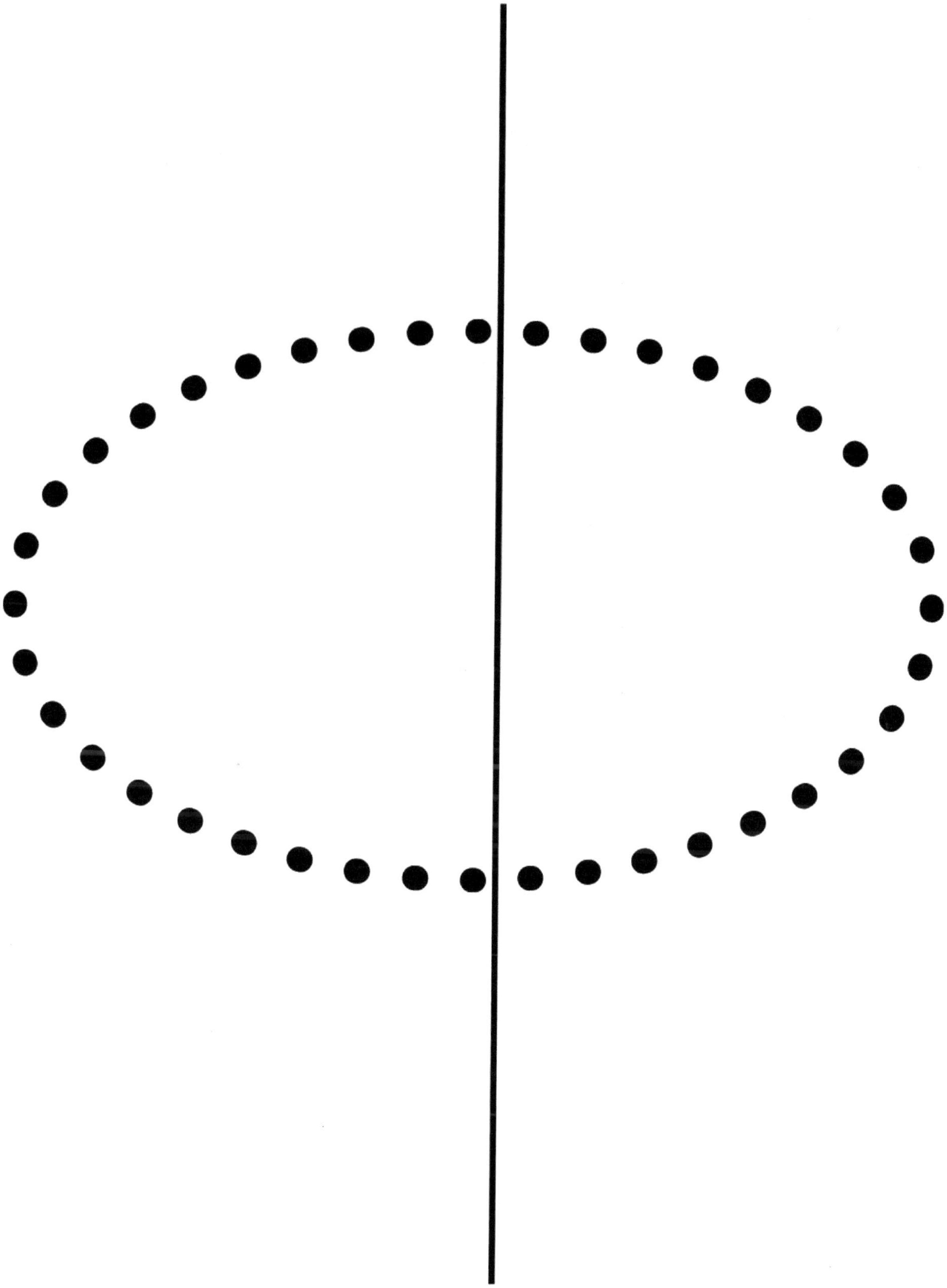

TRACE THE DOTTED LINES TO MAKE SHAPES

FINISH THE PICTURE

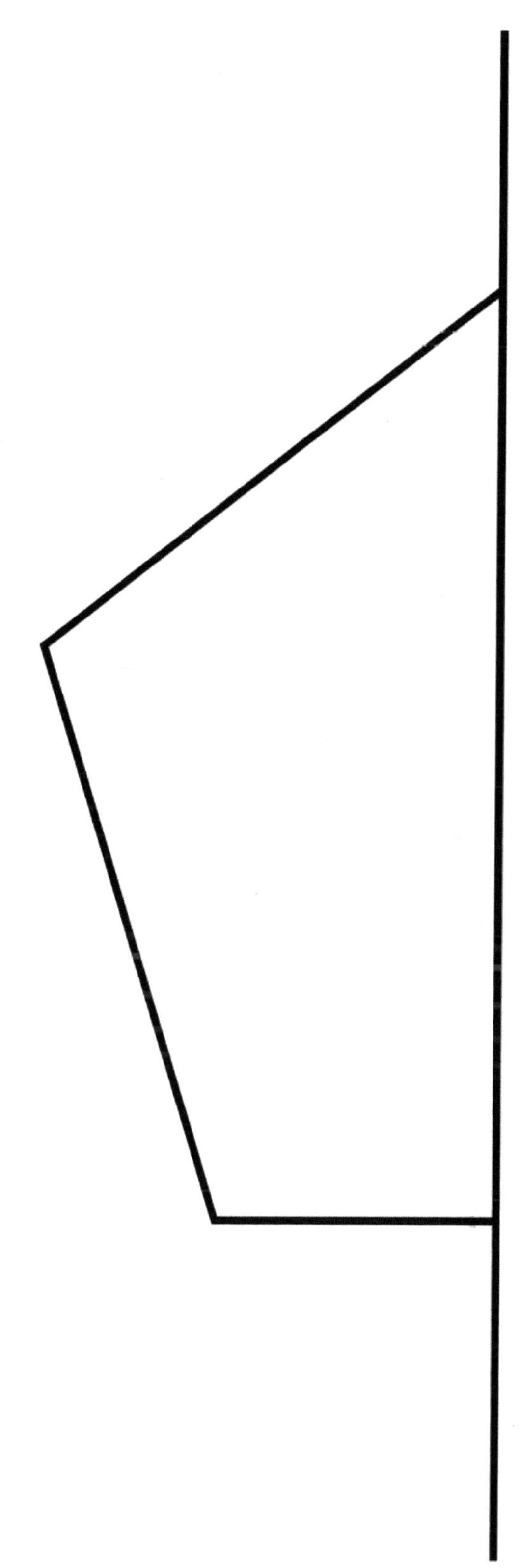

COLOR ALL THE CIRCLES RED

DRAW THE SHAPE WITH BOTH HANDS AT THE SAME TIME

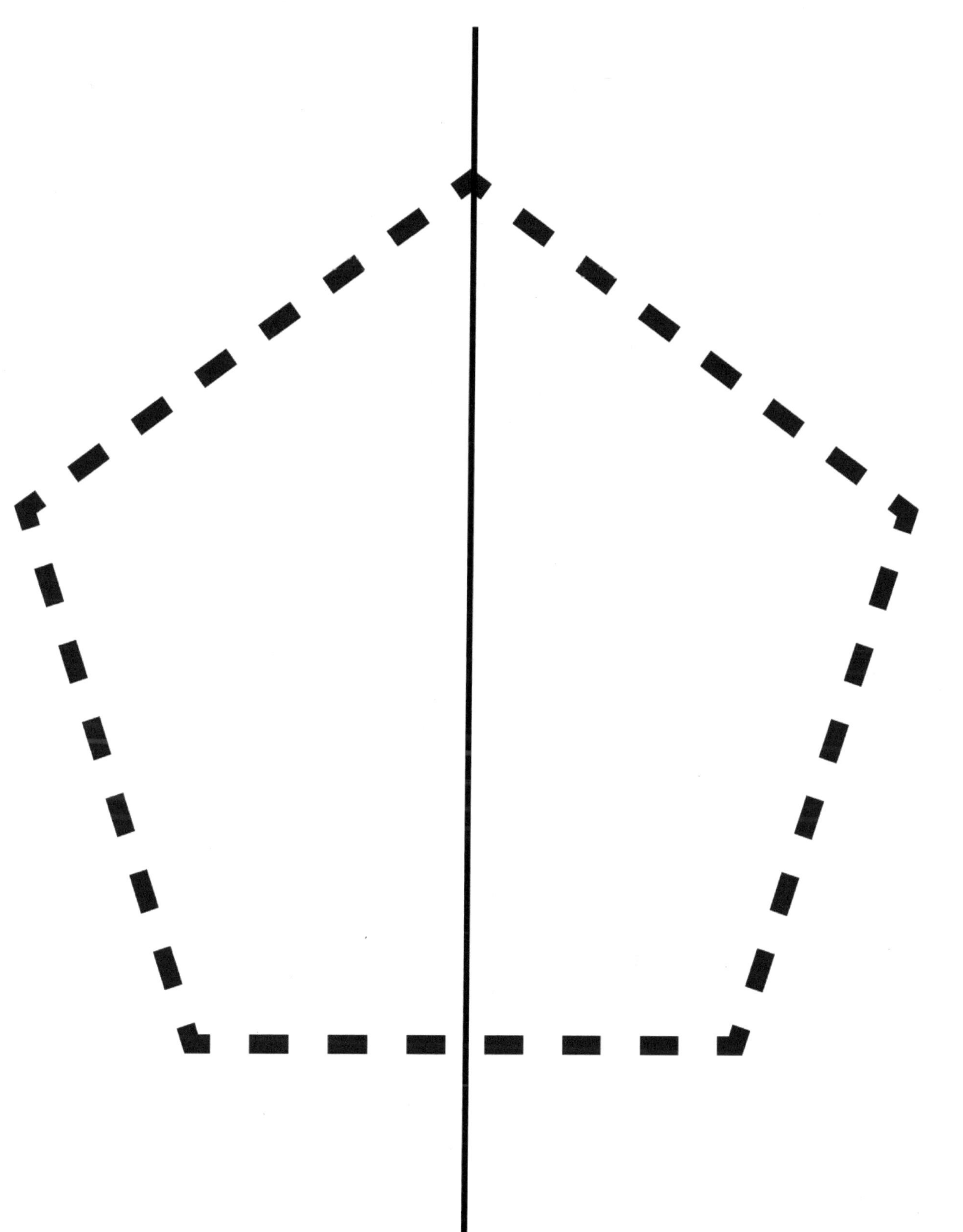

clever projects

HOW MANY SHAPES ARE THERE?COUNT AND WRITE

COLOR THE BABY LION AND HELP HIM TO BLOW BUBBLES BY TRACING THE CIRCLES

FIND THE ROW OF SHAPES IN THE PICTURE BELOW AND CIRCLE IT

WHO IS HIDING BEHIND THE SHAPES?

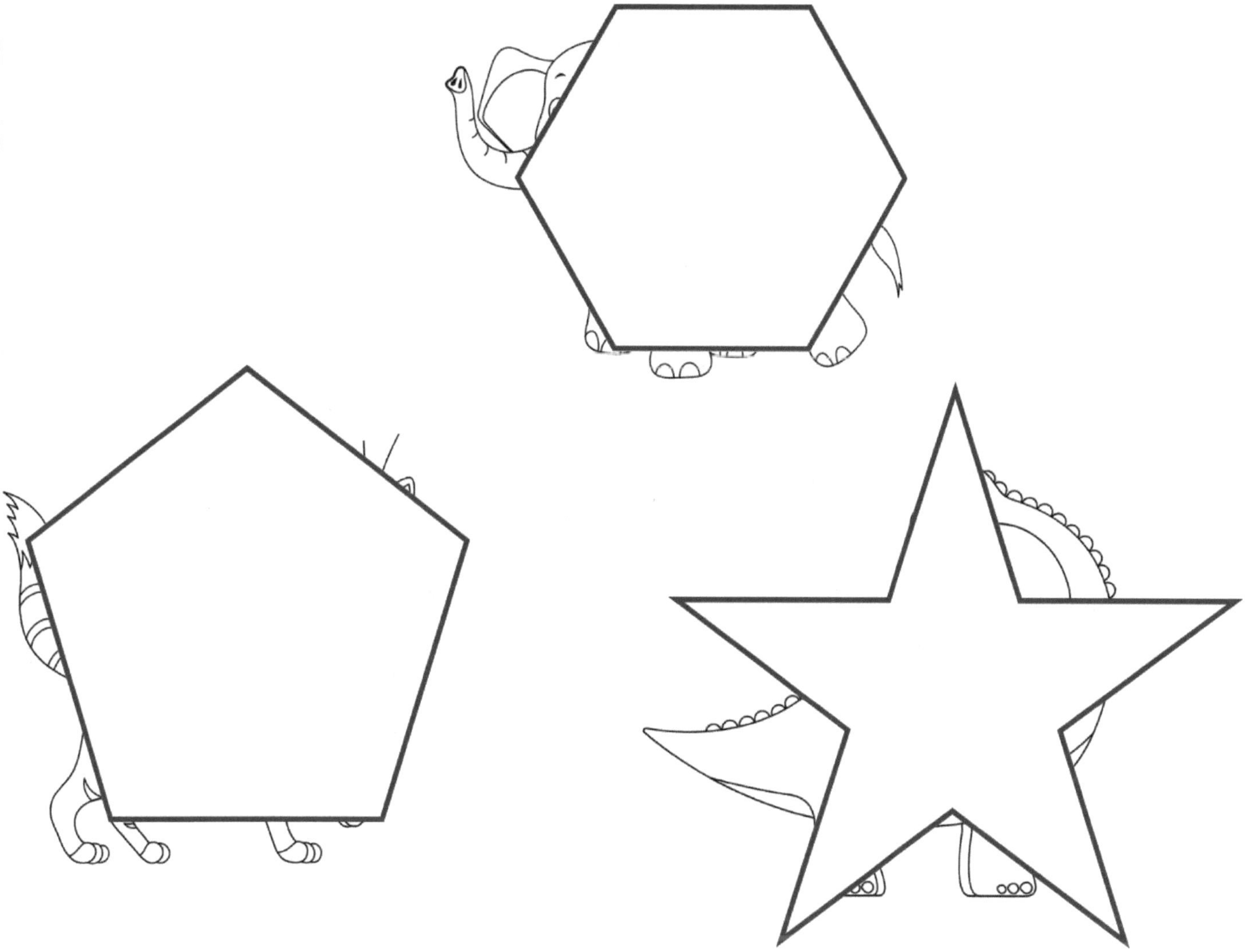

FINISH THE PICTURE

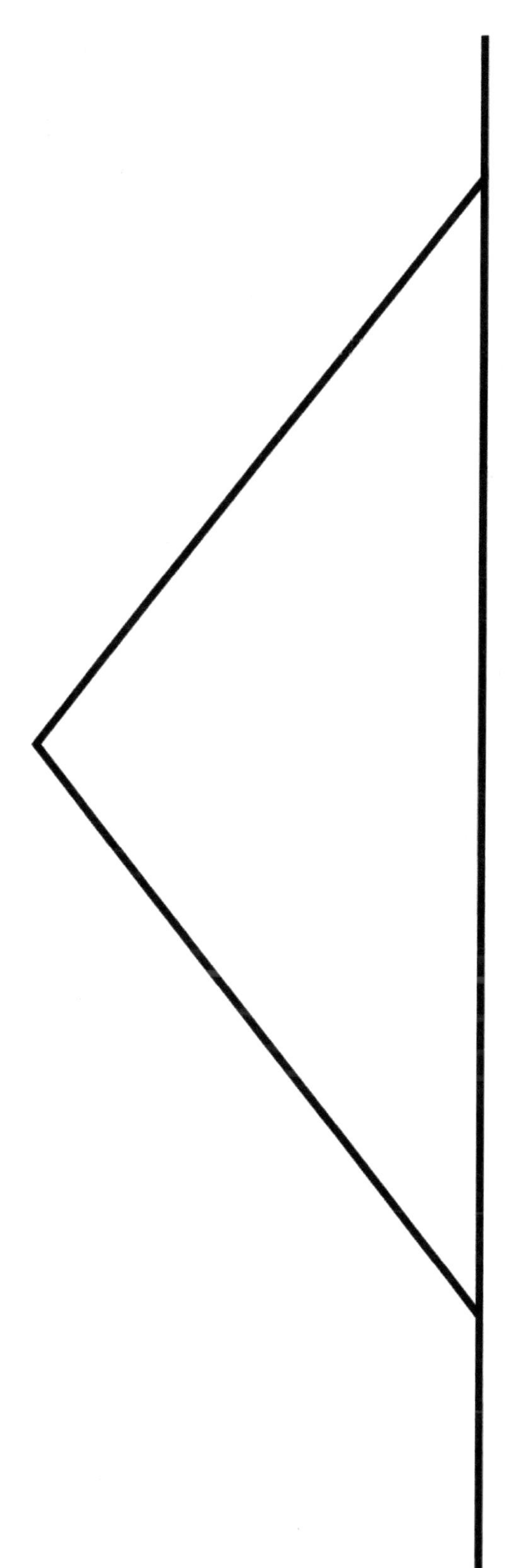

SHAPES GAME

COLOR | TRACE | DRAW

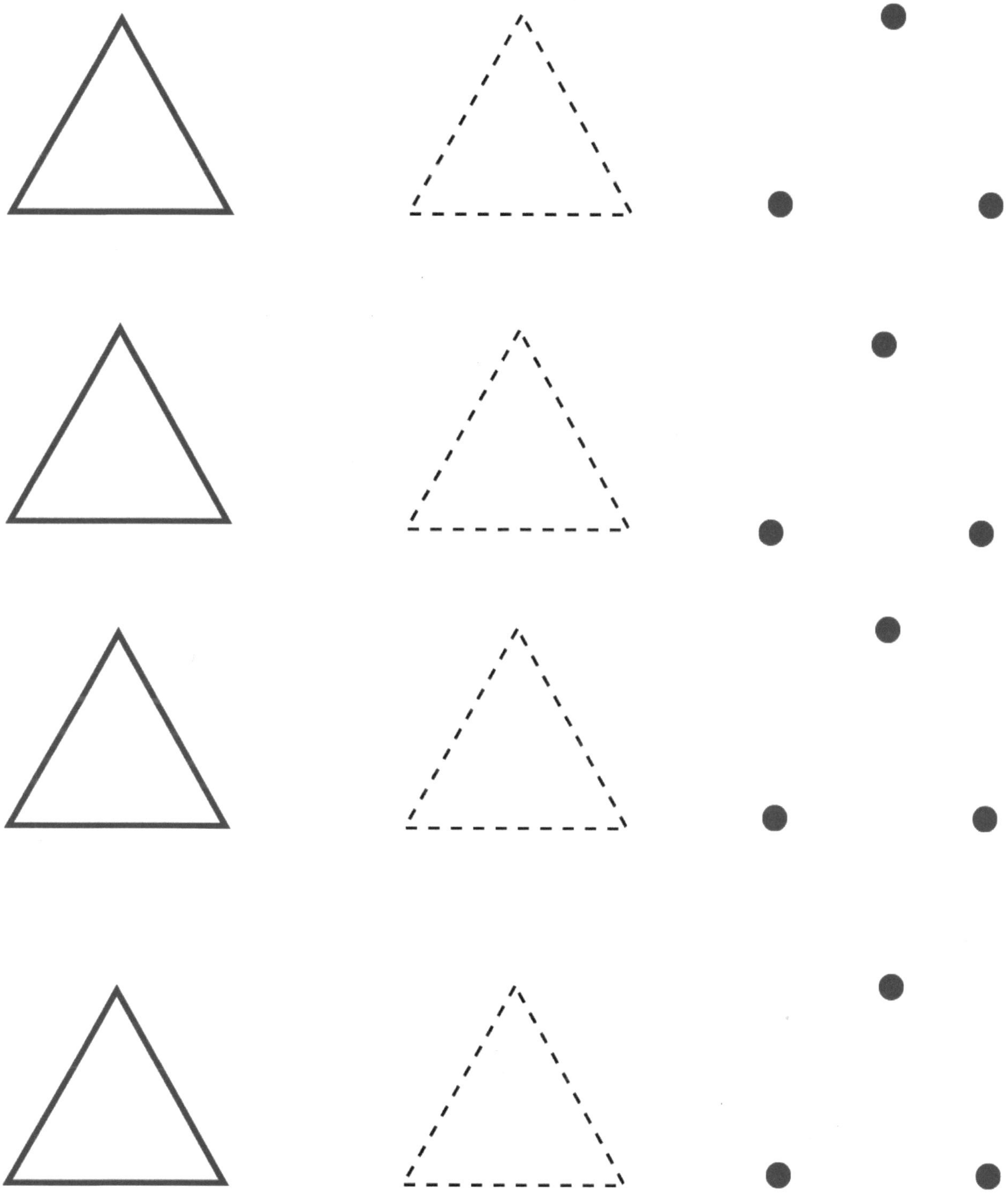

FIND AND COLOR THE SQUARES

CUT THE SHAPE WITH SCISSORS

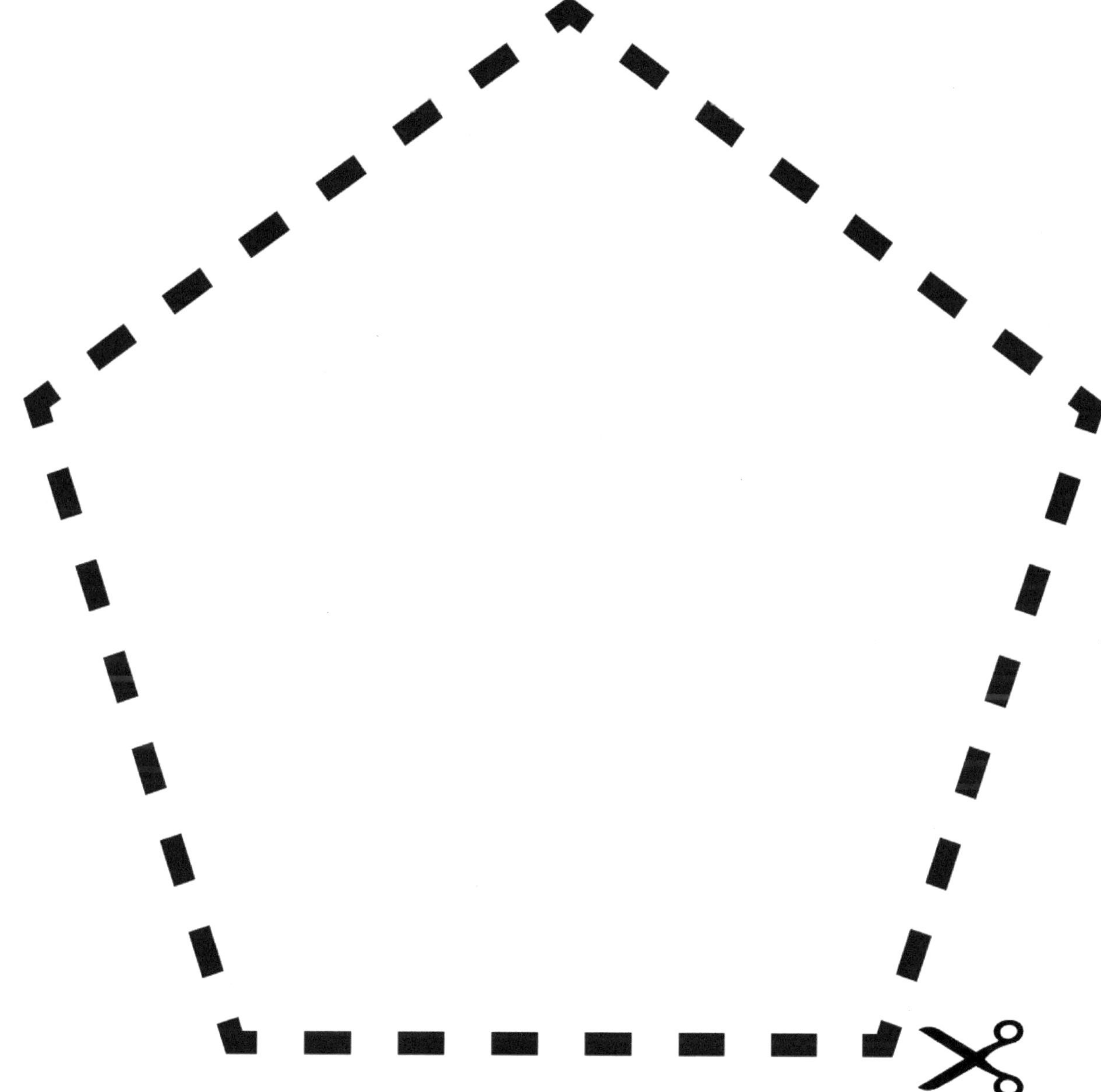

clever projects

COLOR THE DINOSAUR AND HELP HIM TO TRACE THE TRIANGLES

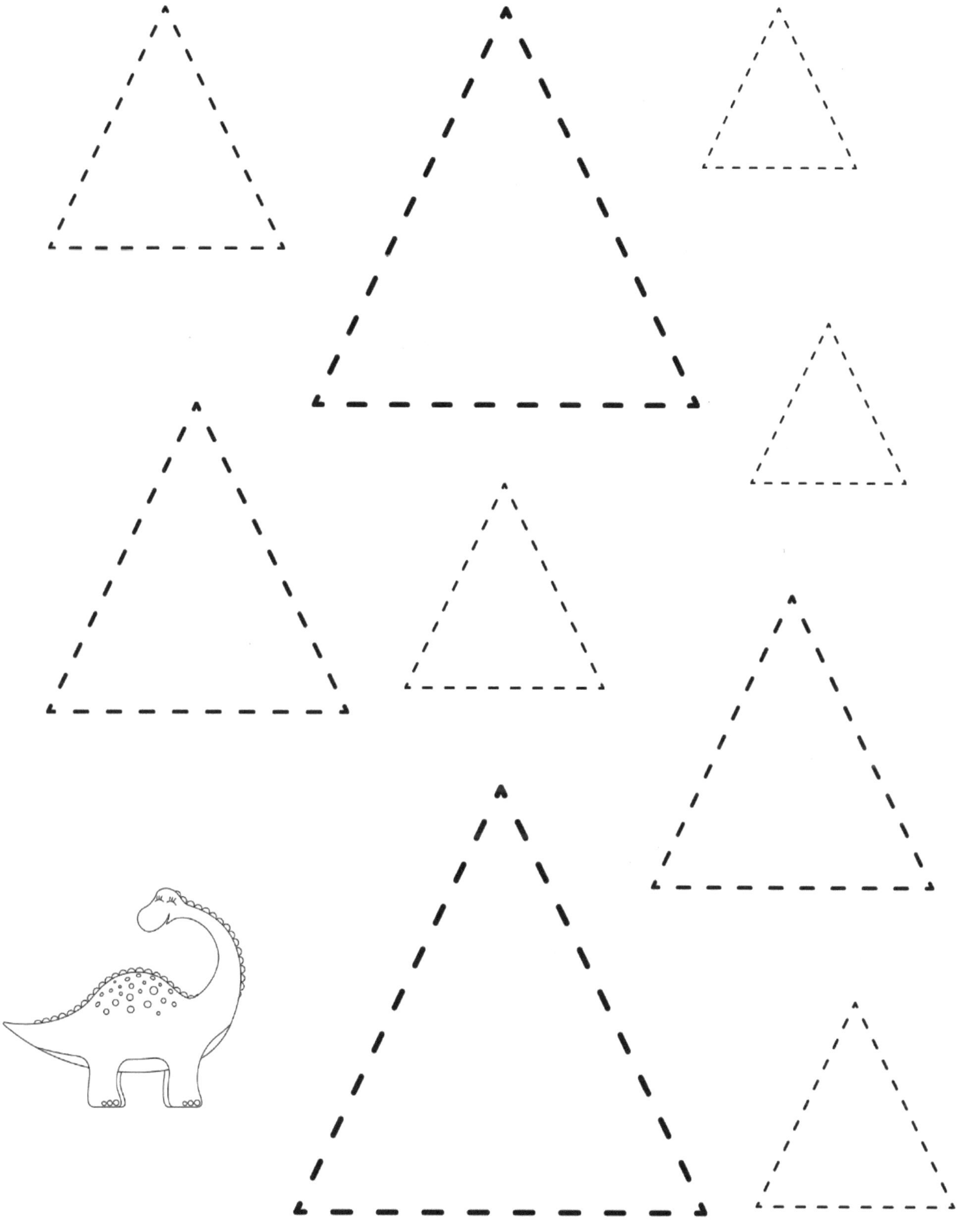

clever projects

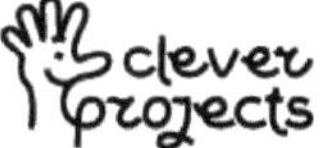

DRAW THE SHAPE WITH BOTH HANDS AT THE SAME TIME

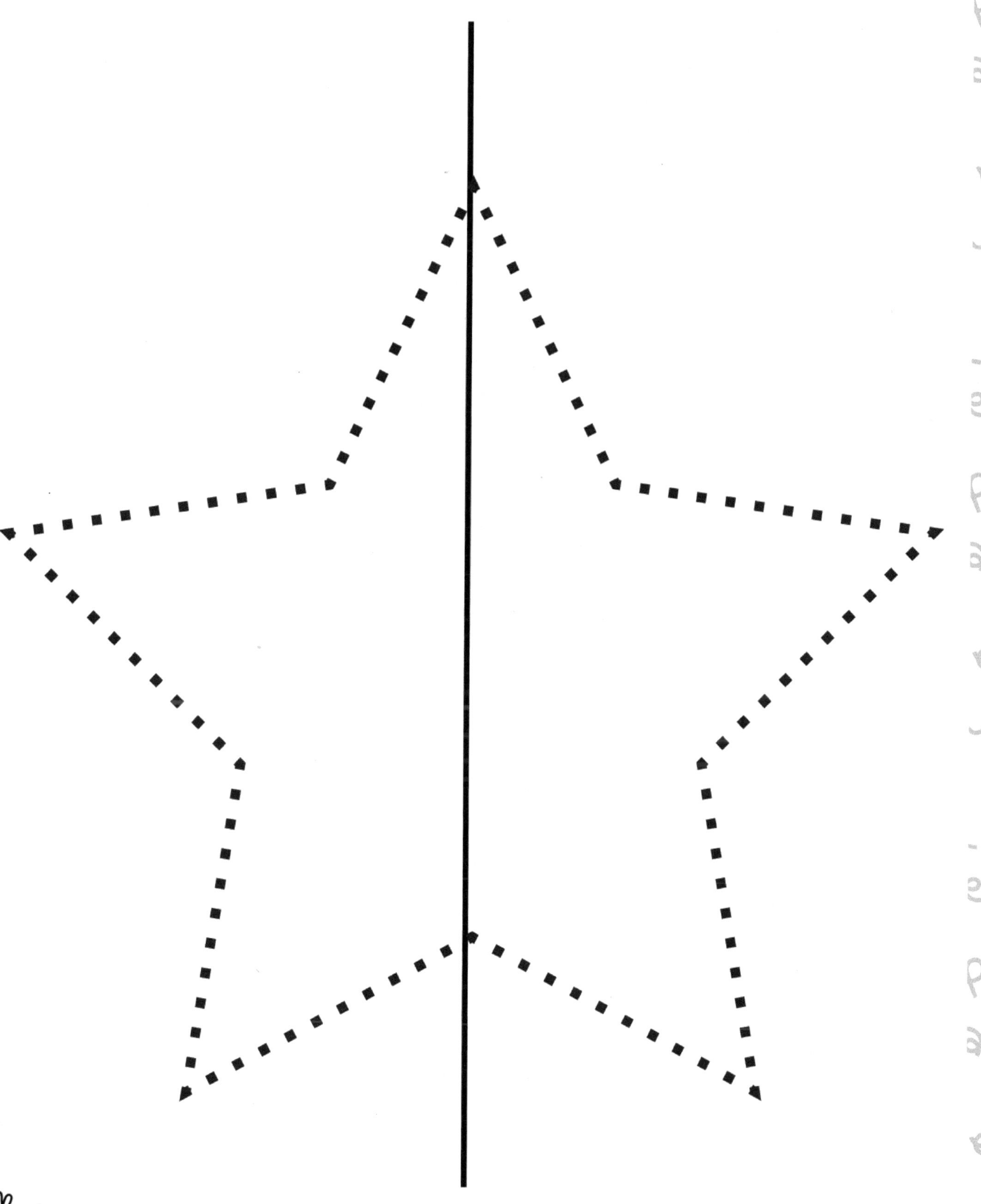

FIND 2 SAME PICTURES IN EACH ROW AND CIRCLE THEM

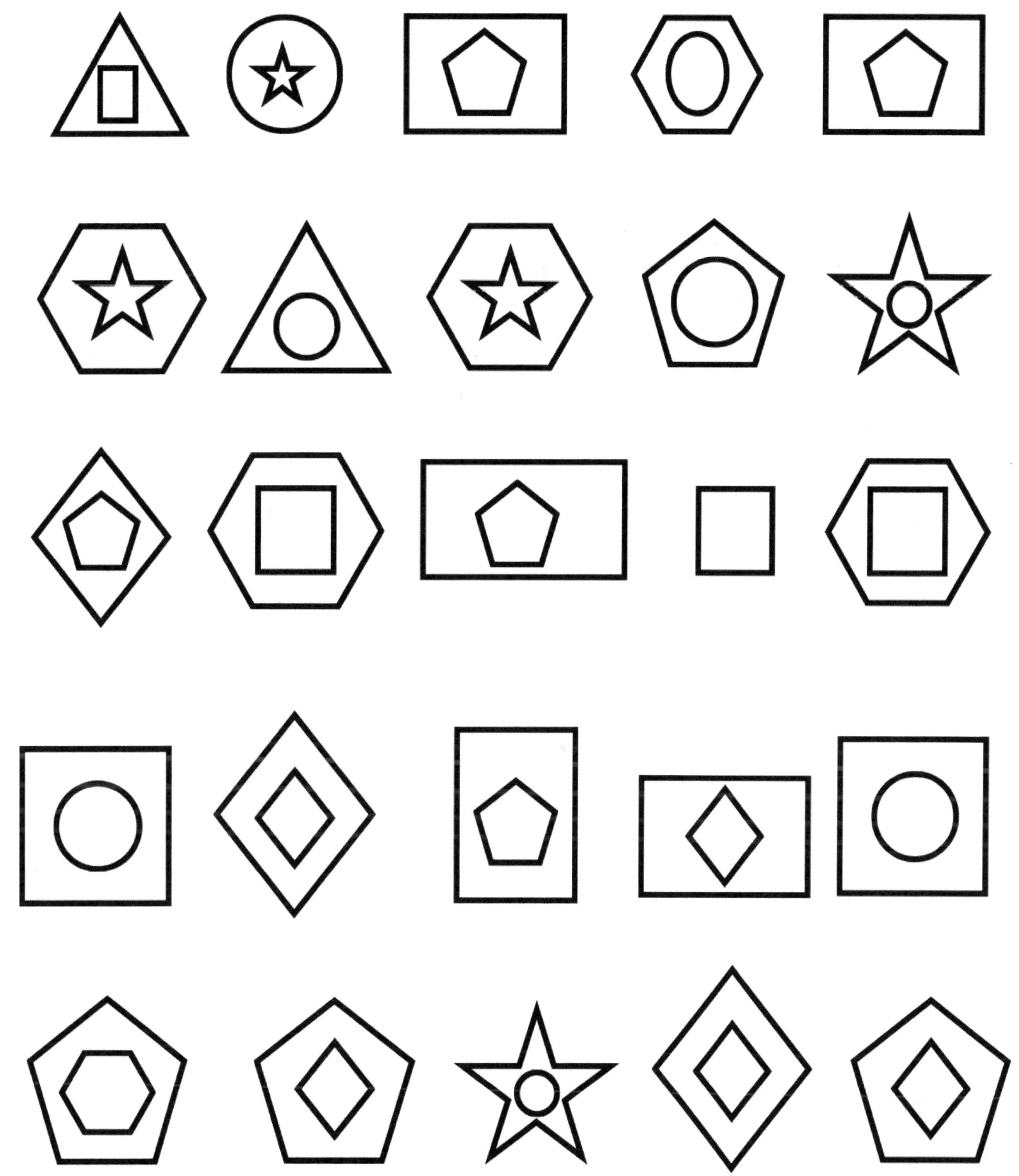

CUT THE SHAPE WITH SCISSORS

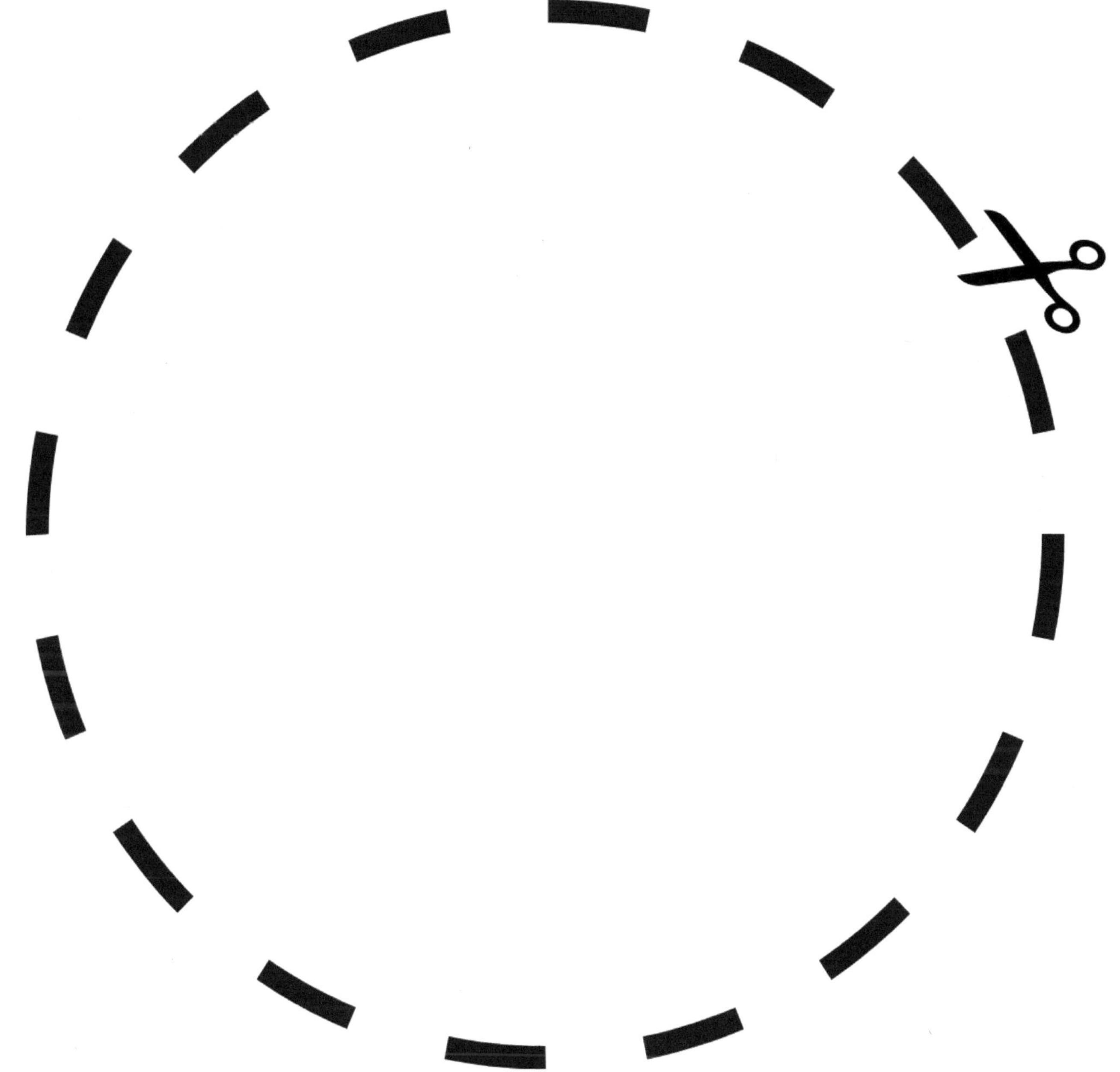

TRACE THE DOTTED LINES TO MAKE SHAPES

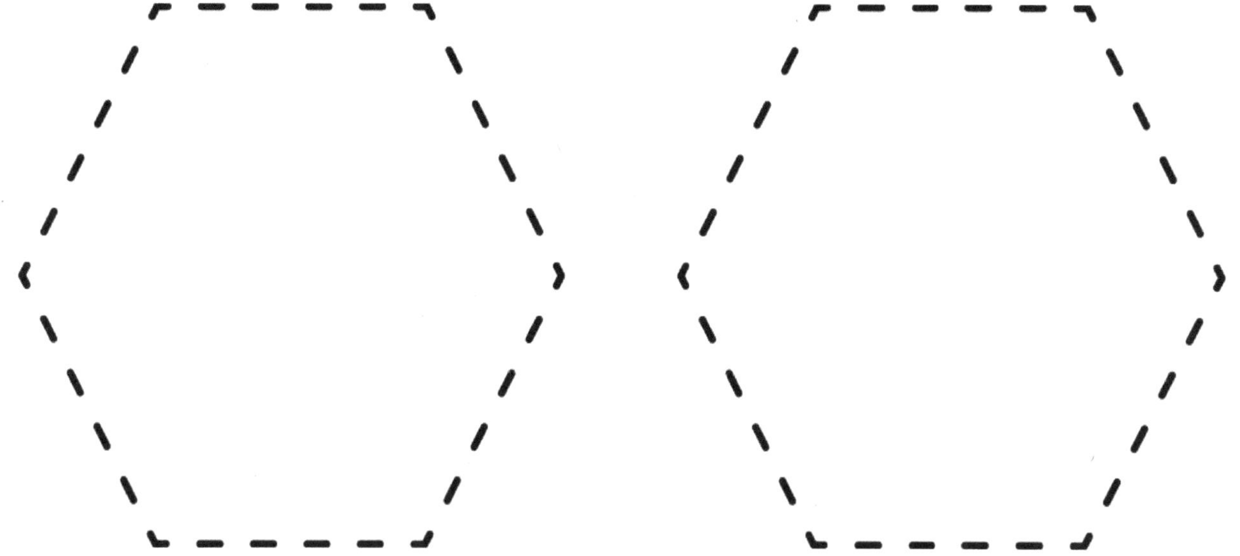

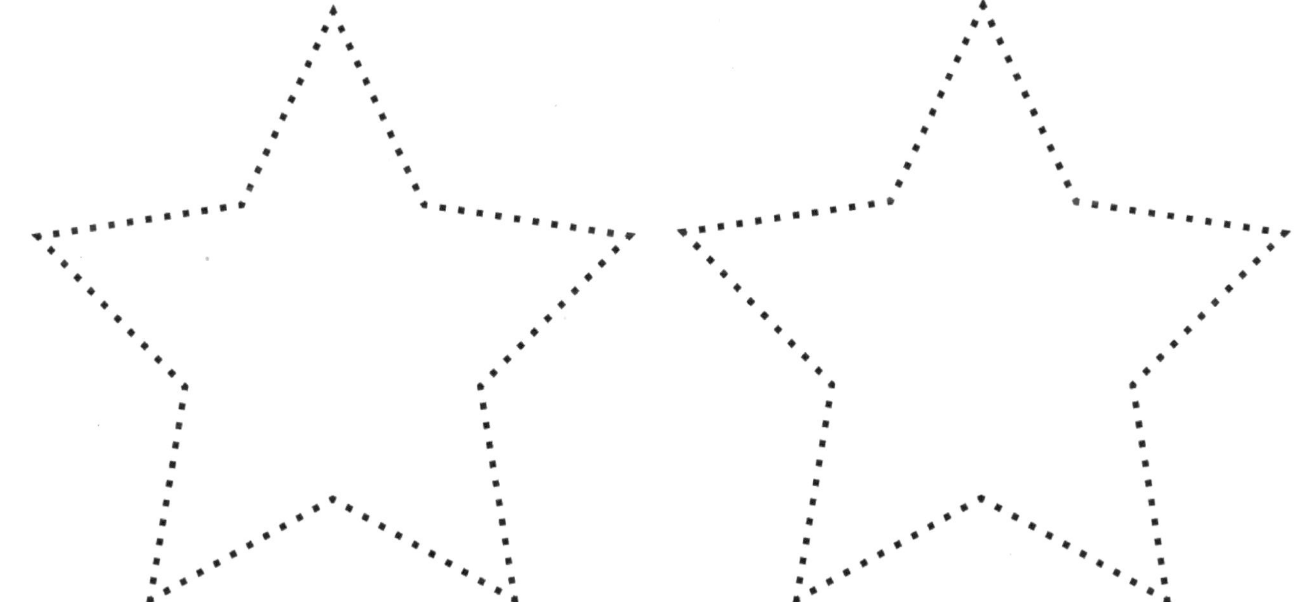

CUT THE SHAPE WITH SCISSORS

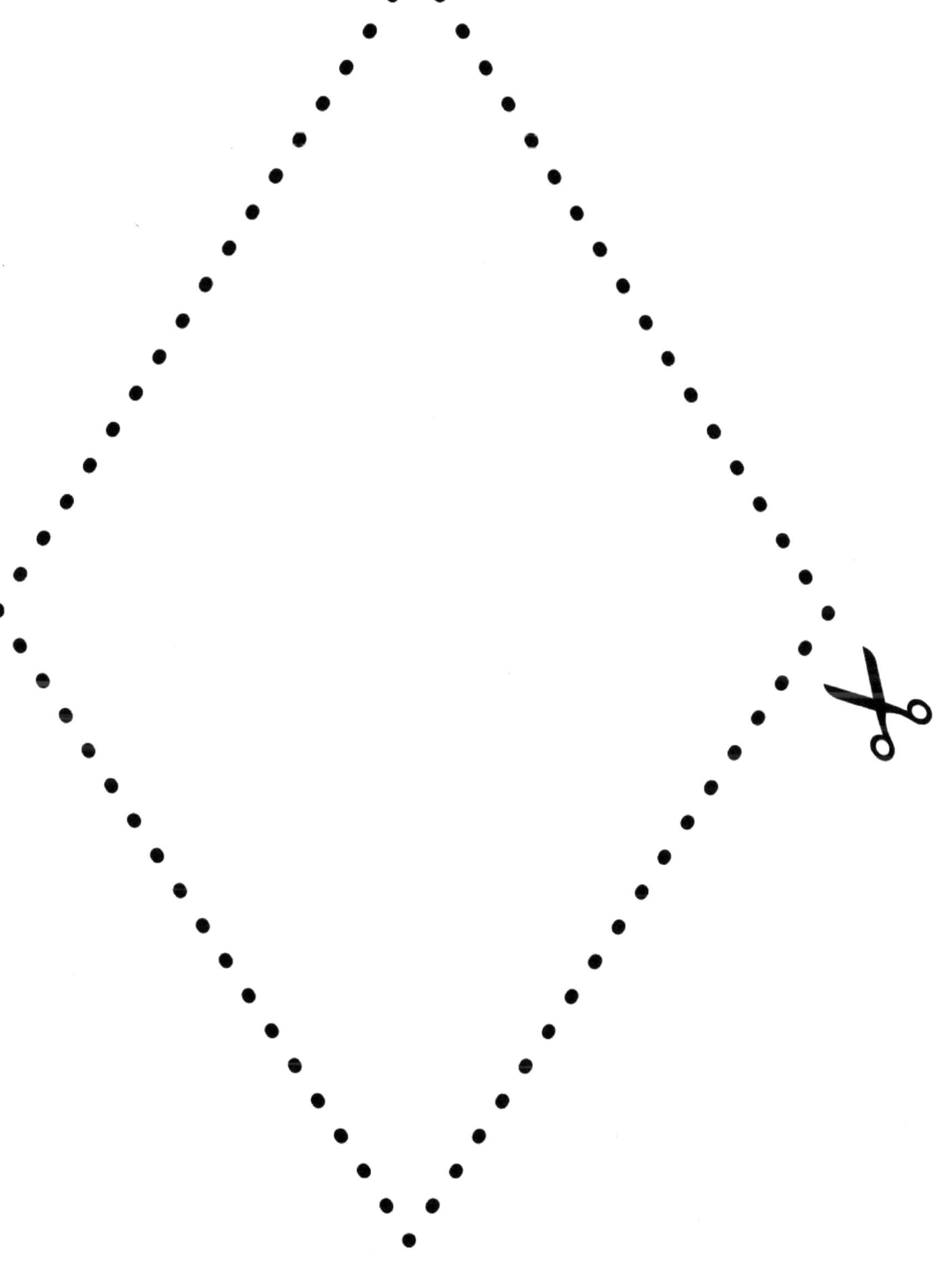

clever projects

WHAT IS HIDING BEHIND THE STAR ?

clever projects

CUT THE SHAPE WITH SCISSORS

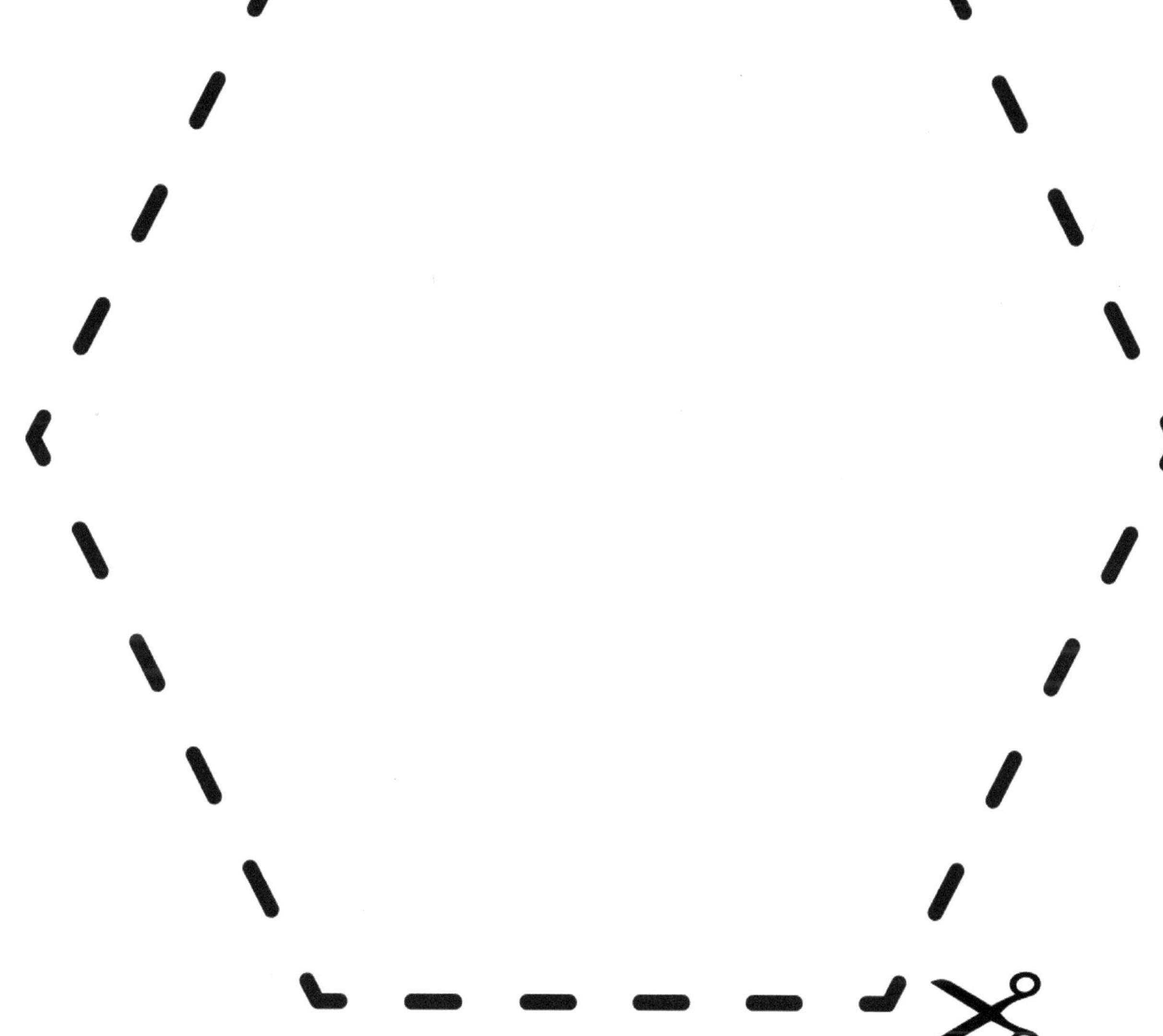

FIND THE ROW OF SHAPES IN THE PICTURE BELOW AND CIRCLE IT

FINISH THE PICTURE

COLOR THE PUPPY AND HELP HIM TO TRACE THE STARS

DRAW THE SHAPE WITH BOTH HANDS AT THE SAME TIME

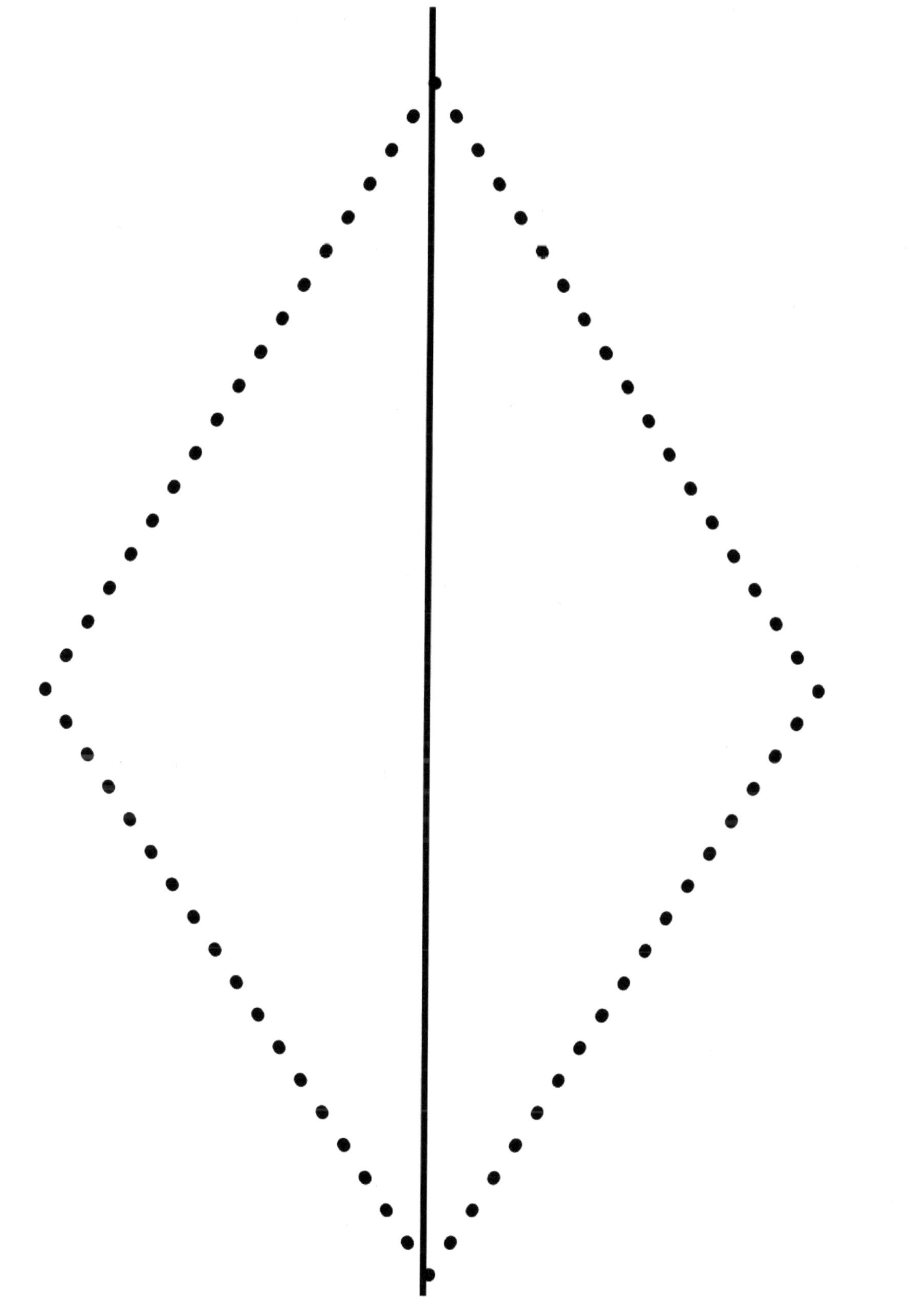

clever projects

HOW MANY SHAPES ARE THERE? COUNT AND WRITE BELOW

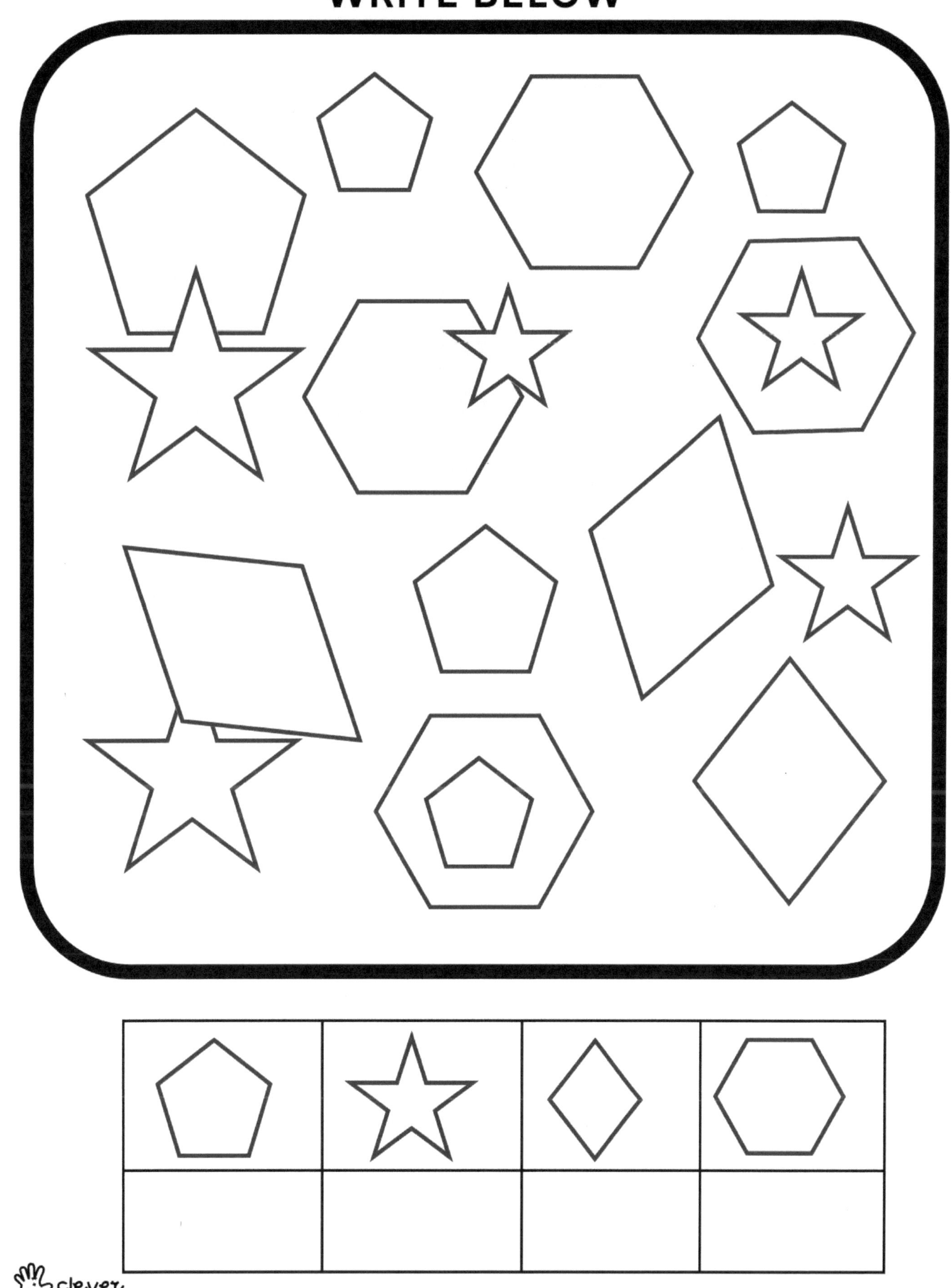

DRAW THE SHAPE WITH BOTH HANDS AT THE SAME TIME

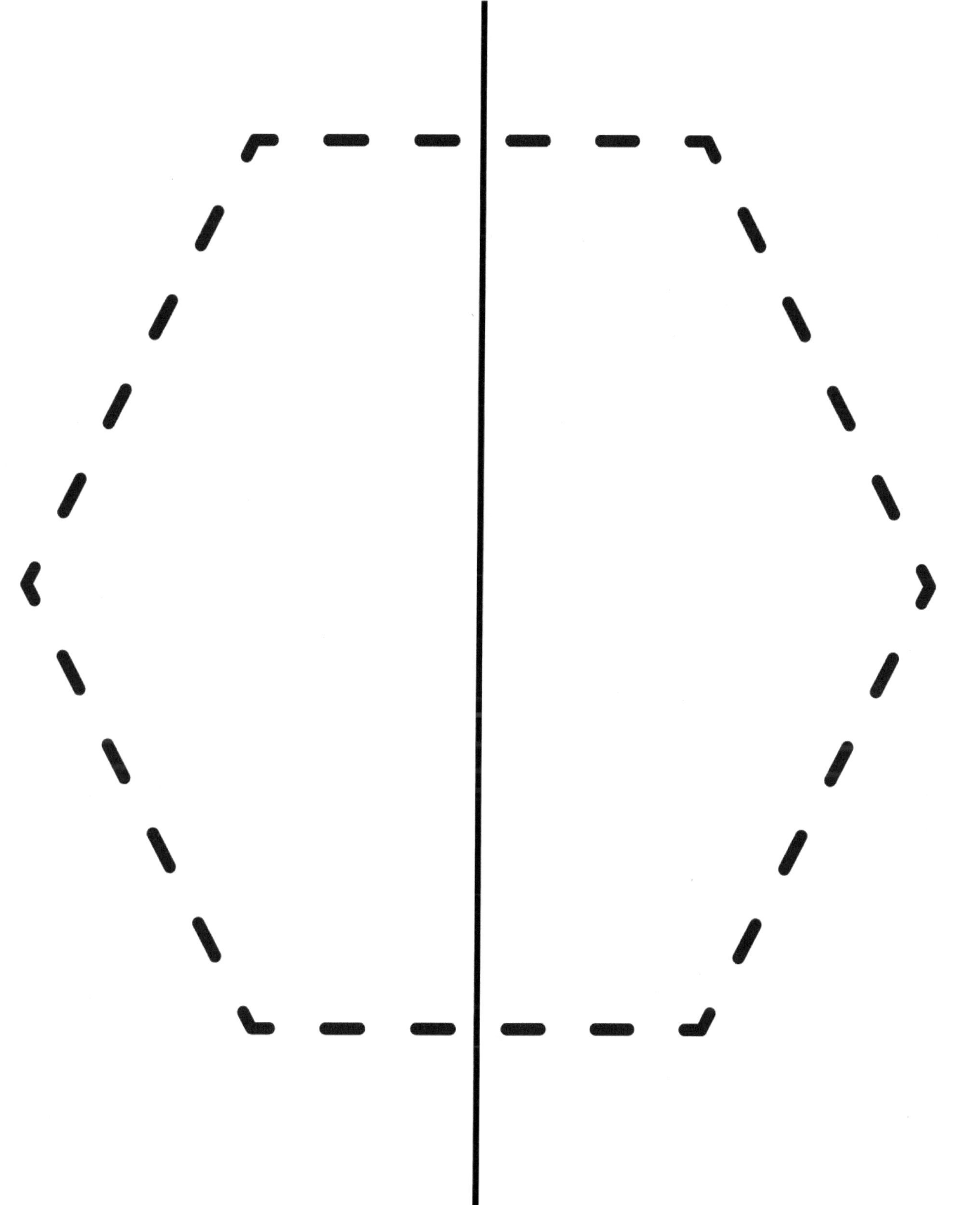

clever projects

TRACE THE DOTTED LINES TO MAKE OVALS

COLOR ALL THE STARS YELLOW, TRIANGLES GREEN

WHAT IS HIDING BEHIND THE TRIANGLE ?

FINISH THE PICTURE

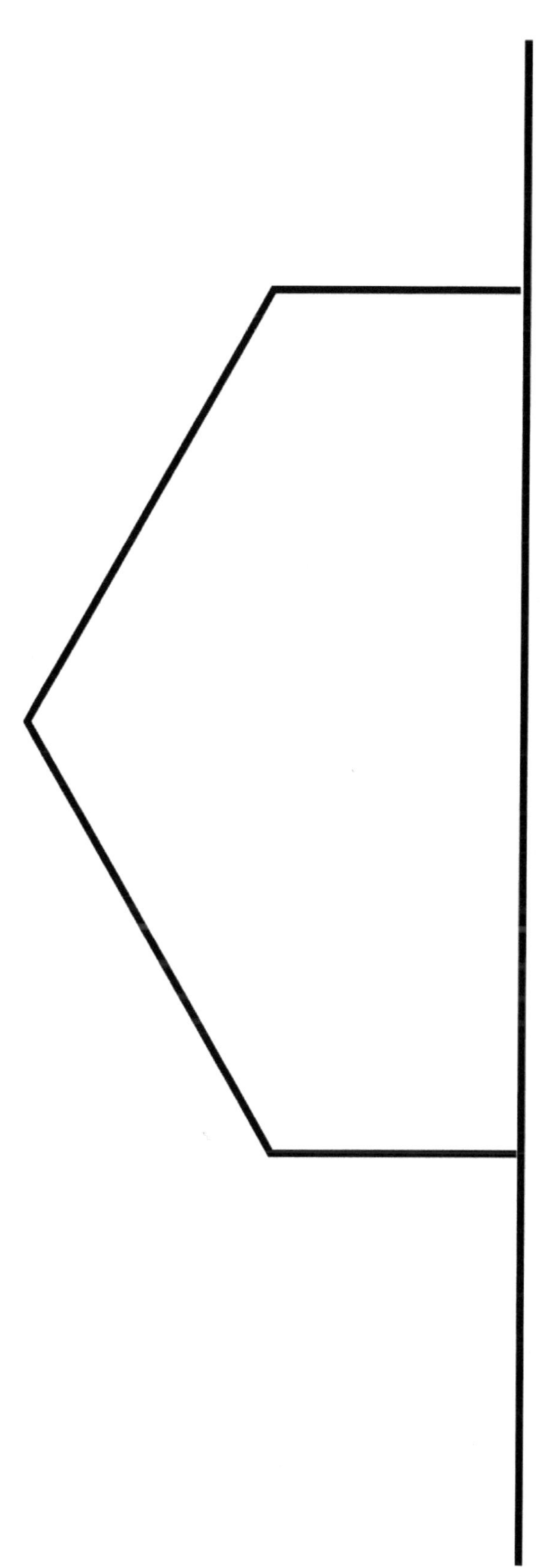

SHAPES GAME

COLOR TRACE DRAW

clever projects

CUT THE SHAPE WITH SCISSORS

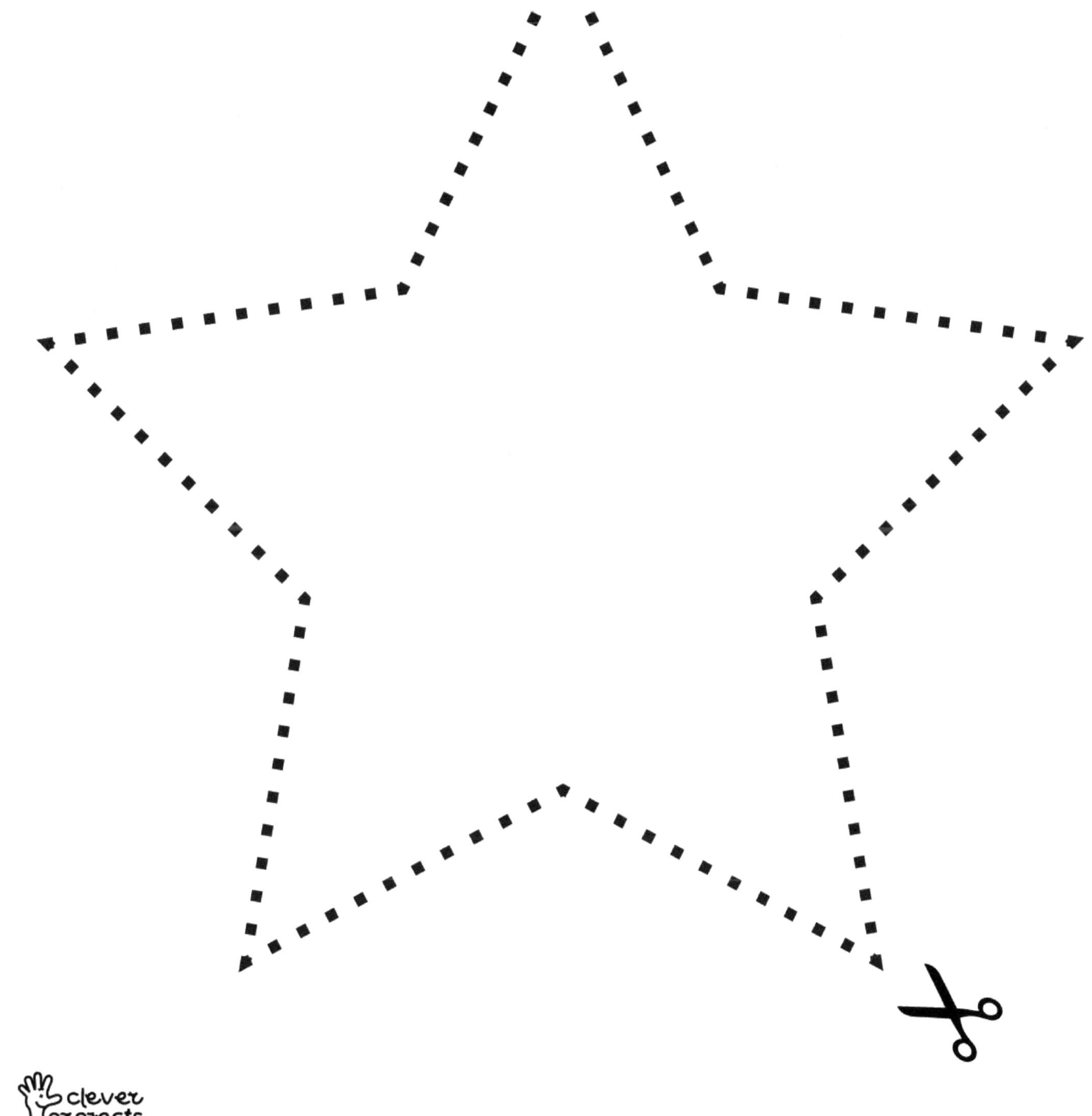

clever projects

FIND AND COLOR THE OVALS

clever projects

FINISH THE PICTURE

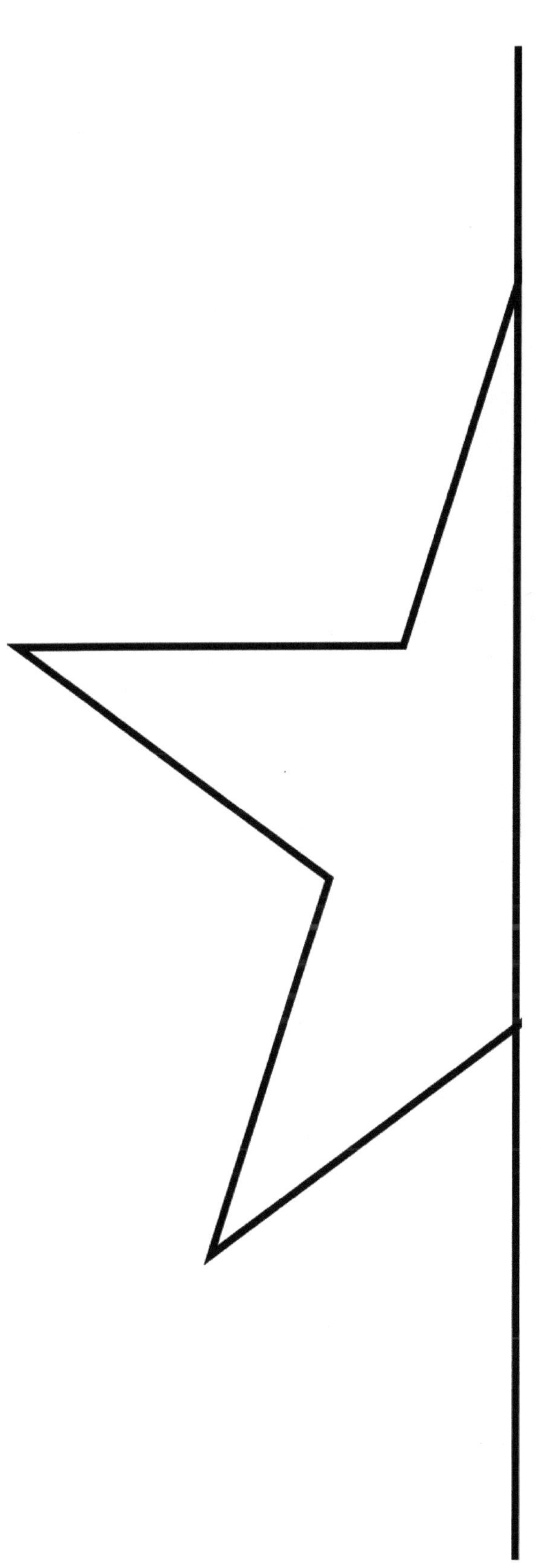

DRAW THE SHAPE WITH BOTH HANDS AT THE SAME TIME

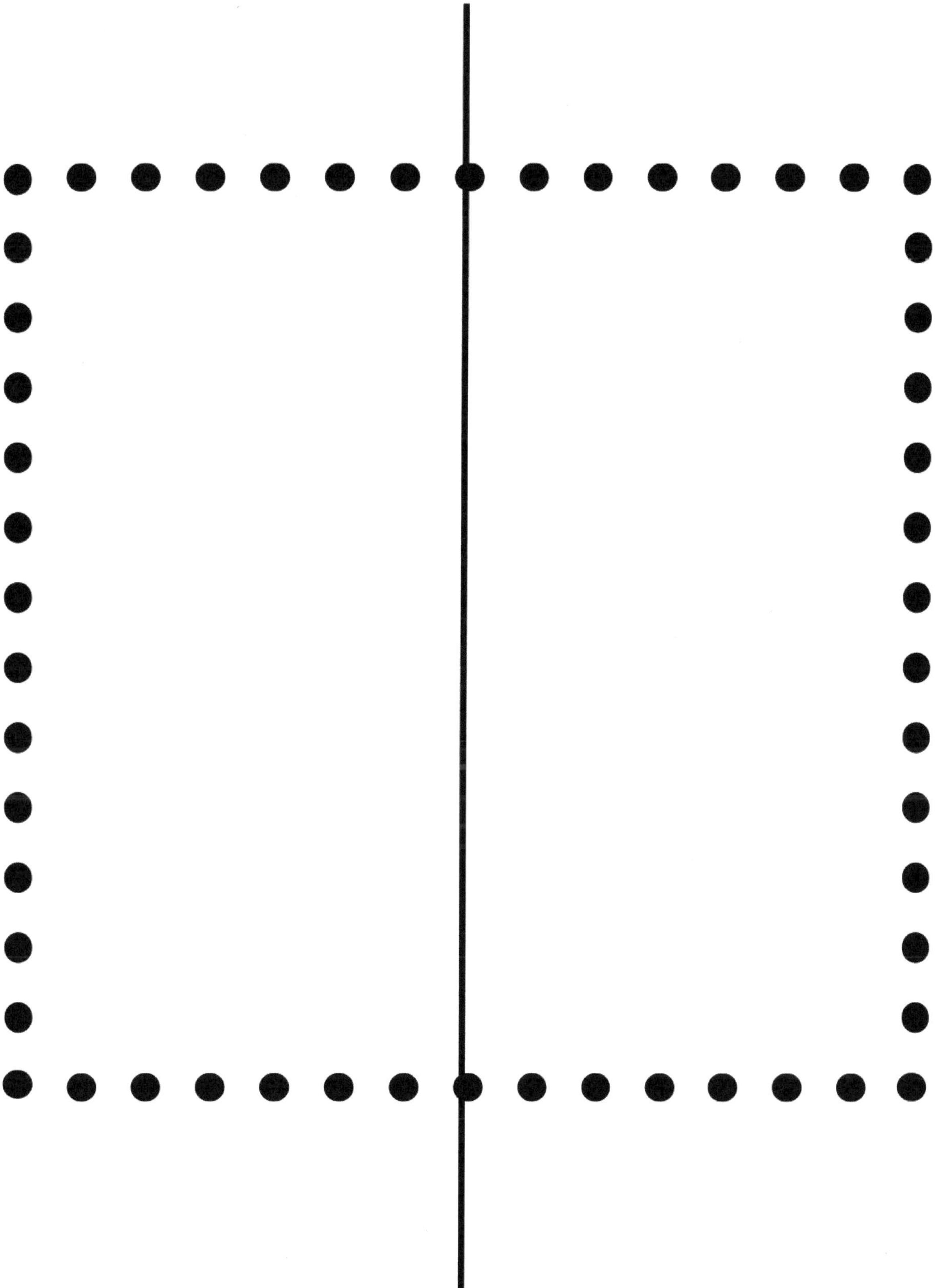

TRACE THE DOTTED LINES TO MAKE PENTAGONS

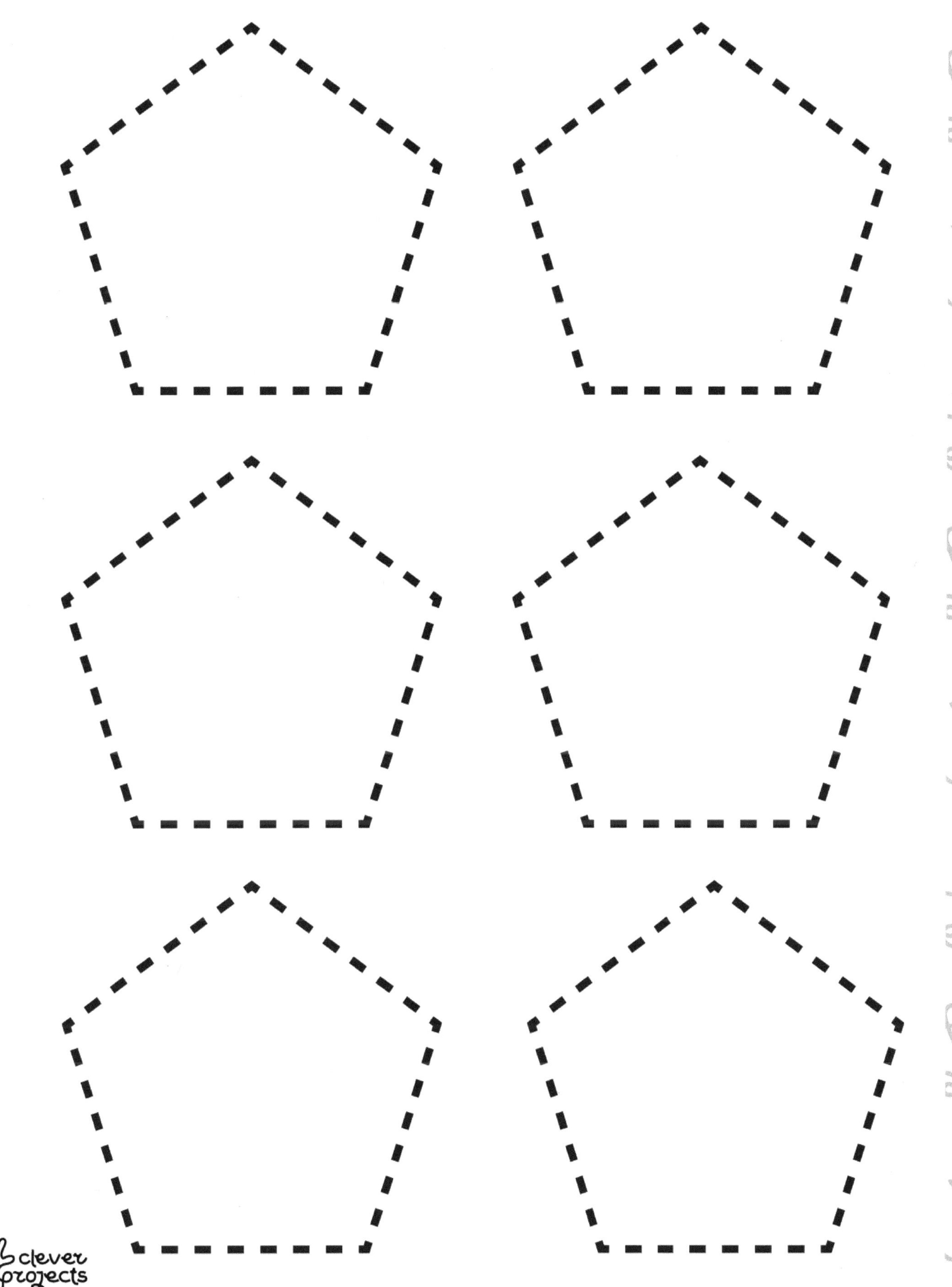

clever projects

CUT THE SHAPE WITH SCISSORS

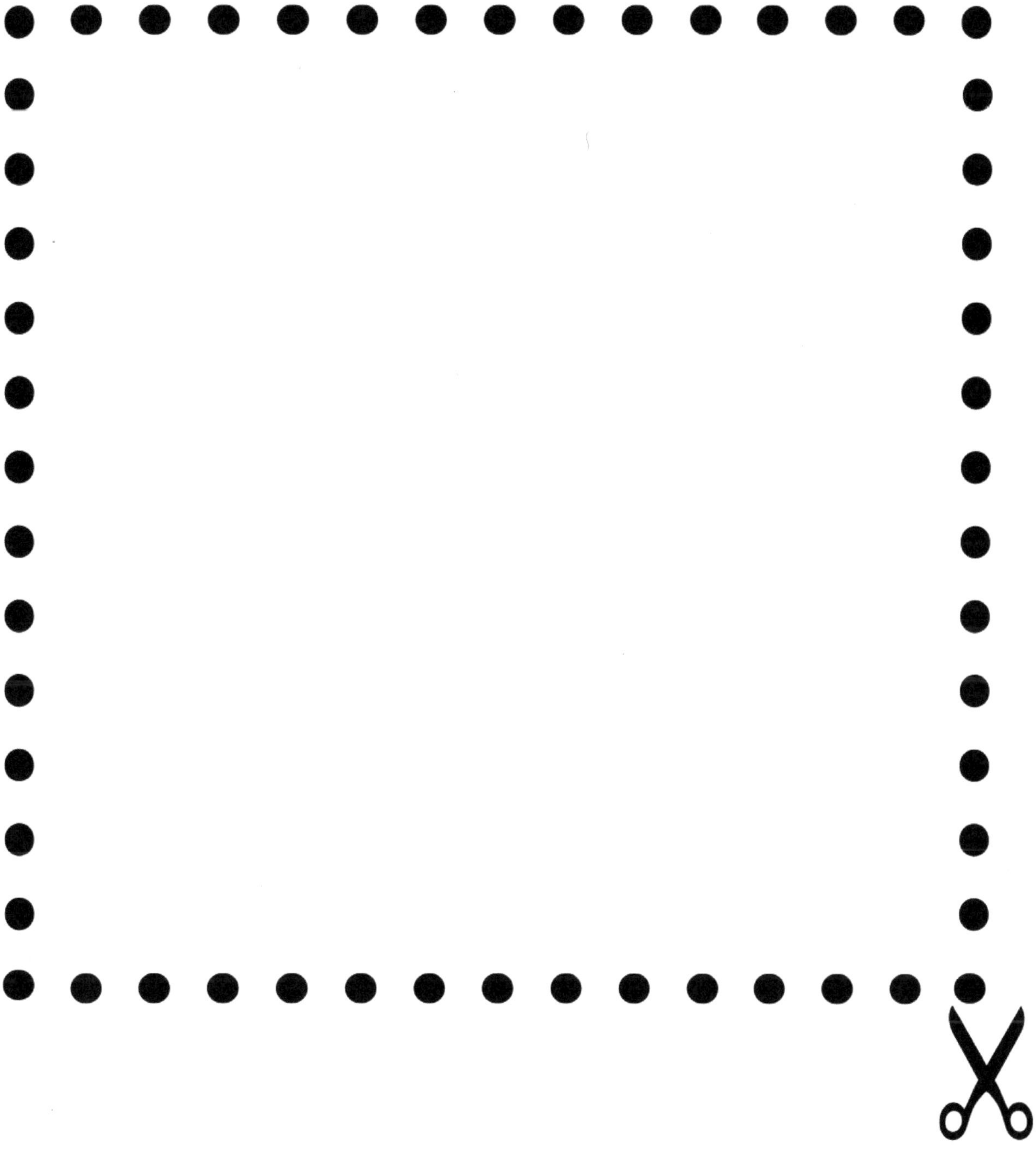

SHAPES GAME

COLOR TRACE DRAW

DRAW THE SHAPE WITH BOTH HANDS AT THE SAME TIME

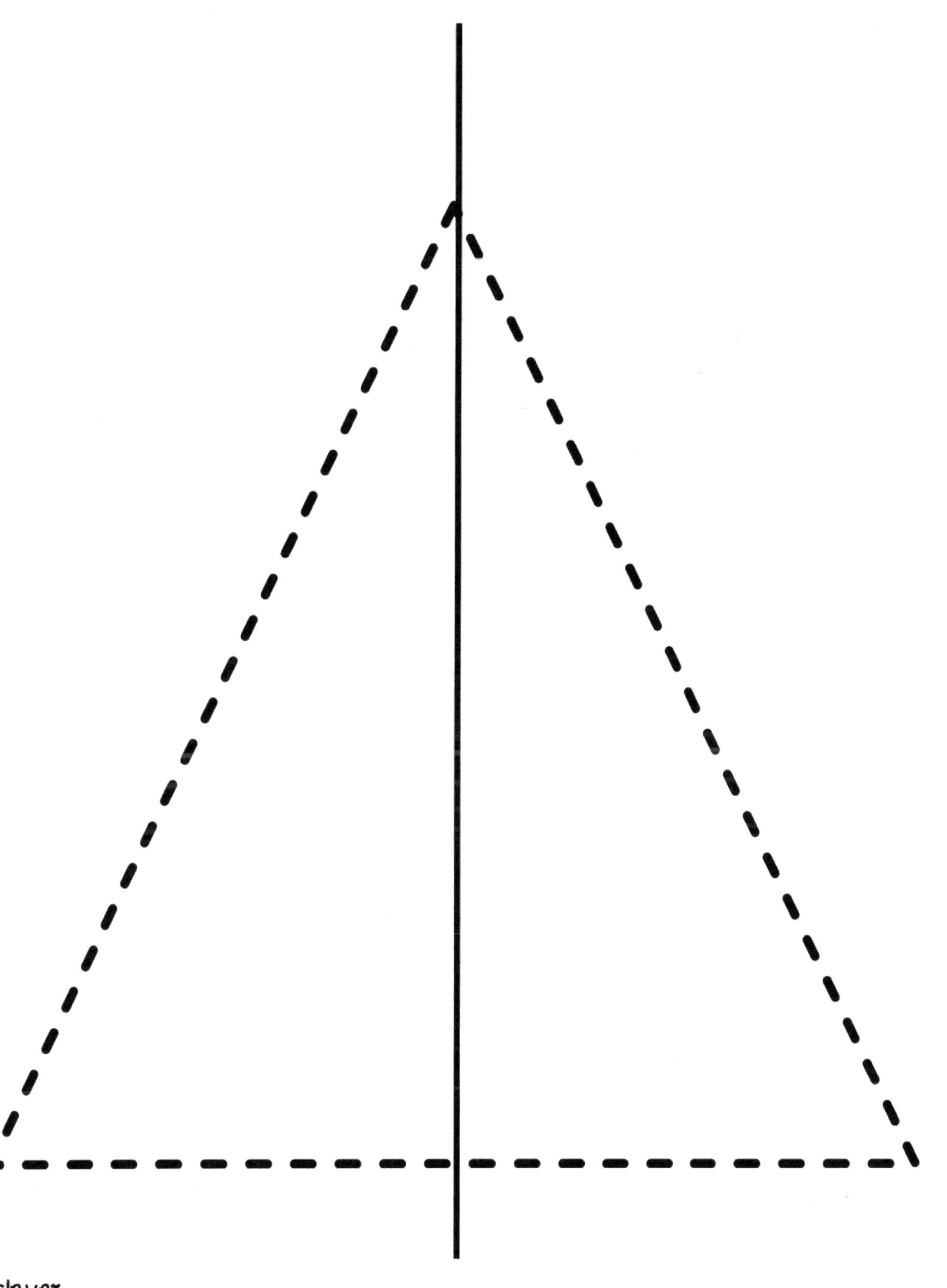

clever projects

FIND AND COLOR THE STARS

TRACE THE DOTTED LINES TO MAKE SHAPES

DRAW THE SHAPE WITH BOTH HANDS AT THE SAME TIME

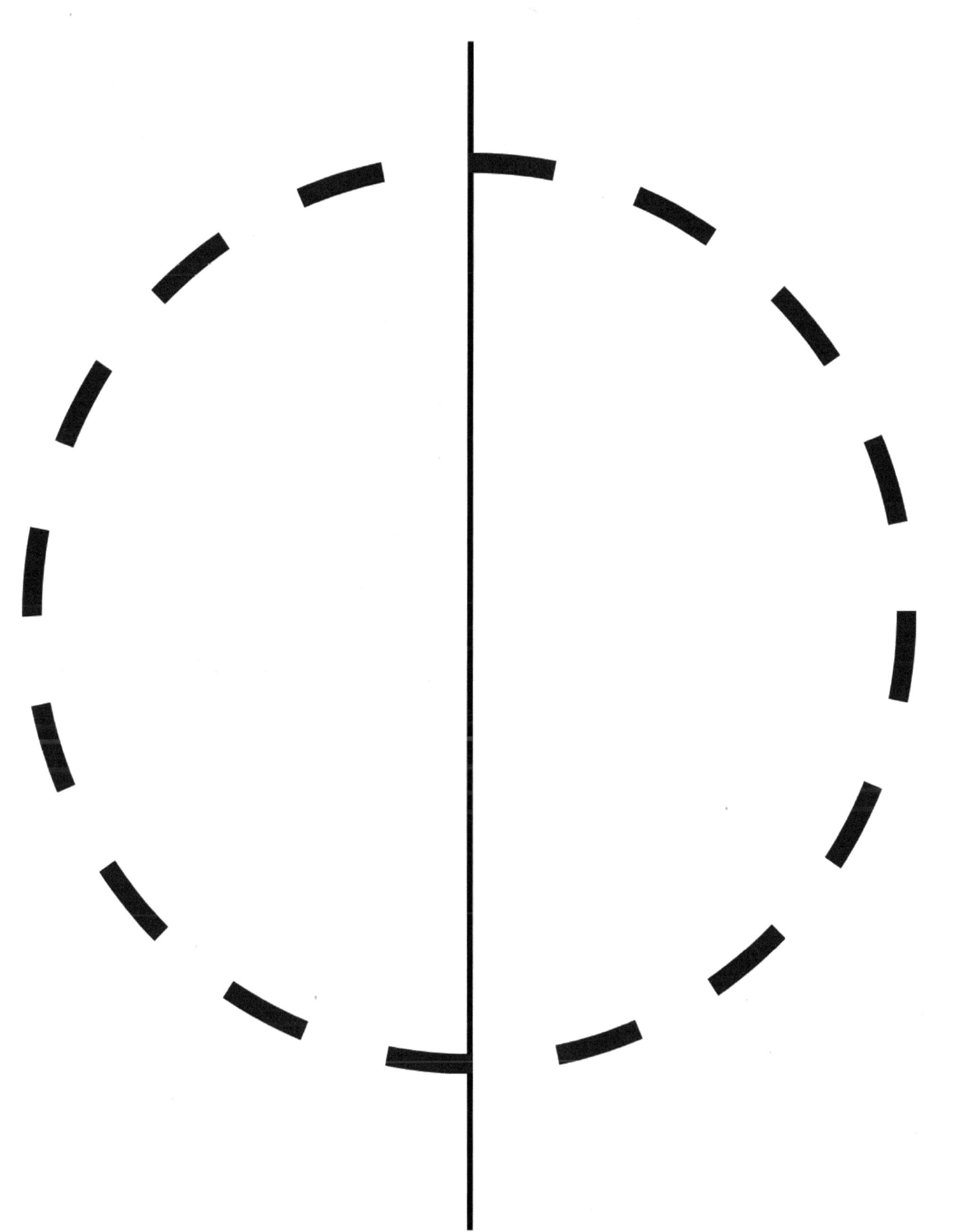

clever projects

COLOR THE BABY HIPPOPOTAMUS AND HELP HIM TO TRACE THE PENTAGONS

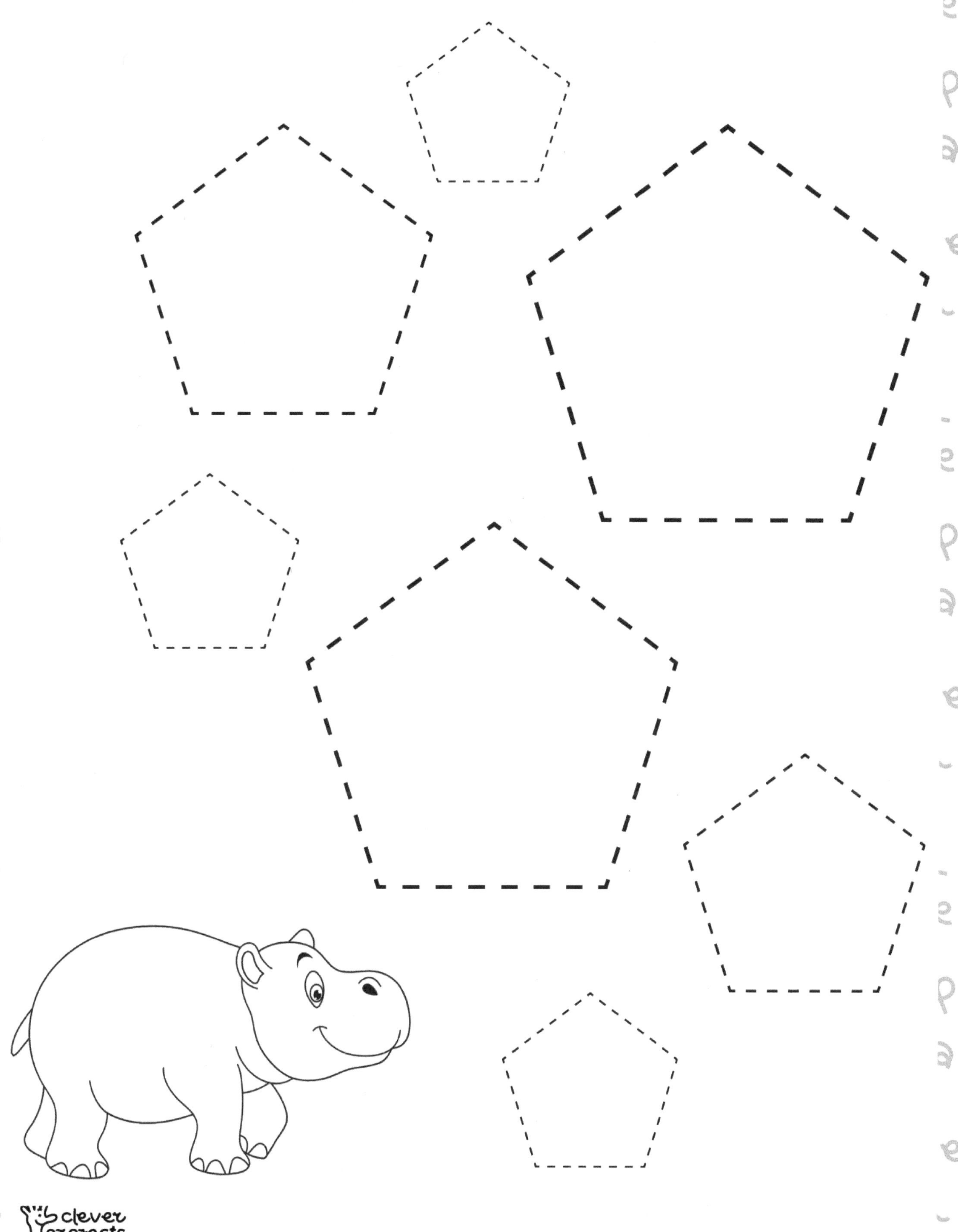

SHAPES GAME

COLOR

TRACE

WHAT IS HIDING BEHIND THE DIAMOND?

CUT THE SHAPE WITH SCISSORS

Printed by Libri Plureos GmbH in Hamburg,
Germany